*Ron and Marilyn
Fisher

January 10, 1990*

GROWING IN STEP

A Christian Guide
To Stepparenting

Dan Houmes
Paul Meier

**today
publishers,
inc.**

2100 North Collins Boulevard
Richardson, TX 75080
(214) 783-7008

©Copyright, 1985 by
Today Publishers, Inc.
2100 North Collins Boulevard
Richardson, TX 75080

ISBN: 0-933629-05-2

Printed in the United States of America

Edited by Marty Williams Anderson

Cover design by Keith Yates

Dedication

This book is dedicated to those stepparents whose desire to grow in step helped to produce this book.

CONTENTS

INTRODUCTION

During the years of my work in marriage and family therapy, nothing has affected me more than the pain of watching marriages end. Divorce was once a rare and obscure occurence. In my childhood it was hardly discussed. Now divorce invades home after home. It even strikes in Christian homes.

I have worked with countless people struggling with the pain and guilt of divorce. Nothing brings more sorrow to the heart of this counselor than to see God's design for happiness disappear in floods of anger, guilt, and resentment.

I have also worked with countless remarriages. There, too, I have shared the pain of remarried people who were struggling to make it work this time. Often, the reason that the remarriage was not working was because of major problems with children. I have shared many of these particular cases in this book, protecting, of course, the identities of the people. Thus, *Growing In Step* is a compilation of several years of counseling experience with stepfamilies and their problems.

I have purposely avoided the divorce issue. As much as I strive to help people save their first marriages, I must face the reality of an exploding number of remarriages. If I have a commitment to people who have remarried, or are considering remarriage, it is to help them make their remarriage the last one. Another divorce helps no one.

Writing this book with the prayer that it will give hope, encouragement, and help to many remarried people, I desire that it will be accepted for that purpose alone. It is not intended to condone a previous divorce. It is intended to stop another one. With these few words of introduction, please open your mind and your heart to *Growing In Step*.

Dan Houmes

CHAPTER ONE

Step by Step

Do you remember when you were a child? Those were the days! Back then

1. The stories all had happy endings.
2. Dad always had a nickel for an ice cream cone from the ice cream vendor.
3. You could always depend on Mom to meet most of your needs.
4. You had parents, siblings and friends around, so you seldom felt lonely.
5. Dad always seemed to have enough money for food and clothes.
6. God was the heavenly version of your father. . . basically someone you asked favors from. And you expected him to answer yes nearly every time.
7. The authority figures in your life (parents, teachers, coaches, church leaders, etc.) loved you and were out for your own best interest.

It's no wonder high-school and college-age youth are so idealistic. They are not yet fully aware of the depths of human depravity. After being educated by the college of "life's hard knocks," most of these idealistic youths will wake up to a real but disappointing world where:

1. *Some* stories have happy endings, but many are tragedies.
2. Dad ran out of nickels for ice cream cones.
3. Mom is not around to take care of you any more.

4. You frequently feel lonely and sometimes abandoned. You may even feel that if you died, nobody would really care that much.
5. Dad ran out of money for food and clothes. You're on your own now!
6. God has not come through for you the way you expected Him to. He let some loved one die whom you still needed; He let your mate leave you for another lover; He allowed your friend or child to develop an incurable disease or handicap; He left you struggling for financial survival. In short, you can't depend on God to do what *you* tell Him to do (like you thought you could when you were a youth).
7. The authority figures now in your life (bosses, landlords, police, IRS, etc.) seem to be interested only in themselves. Your acceptance by them is purely conditional, based totally on your ability to perform up to *their* expectations. You exist to meet *their* needs. If you fail, you are rejected!

Welcome to the real world!

We are living in an age where the divorce rate is:
1. 40 percent for first marriages.
2. 60 percent for second marriages.
3. 80 percent for third marriages.
4. 90 percent for fourth marriages.

In this real world we are living in, most people do *not* learn much from a marriage failure. Instead, they tend to marry another mate similar to the first one (who had faults similar to Daddy's), and the cycle goes on.

As a psychiatrist, I have seen this pattern literally

thousands of times. I once treated a movie actress who had been married six times. All six of her husbands seemed nice when she married them, but all six ended up running around on her and abusing her either physically or verbally. They all abused either drugs or alcohol.

I remember predicting during our first session together that she had grown up with a father who:

1. was probably an alcoholic
2. ran around on his wife (her mother)
3. ignored her most of the time
4. physically abused her at times
5. sexually molested her as a young teenager

The thirty-year-old actress jumped back in amazement and confessed that all five of my predictions were true. She said that she had never told anyone about her father molesting her. She wondered how in the world I could have guessed that. In reality, the five guesses I made were very logical to an experienced psychiatrist who sees the same patterns over and over again. Her body language (mannerisms, seductive clothing, etc.) also gave her past away to me.

Through long-term therapy and through the development of a realistic relationship with Christ and His world, she gained many insights, changed many decisions, and learned finally how to bring to her own life a more happy "ever after."

Part of *reality* is the fact that:
in spite of the depravity in the world;
in spite of loneliness;
in spite of major disappointments and set-backs;
in spite of rejection by a mate or by parents;
in spite of financial struggles;

11

in spite of conditional acceptance by authority
figures;

in spite of fears of personal failure;

in spite of sometimes overwhelming feelings of
sadness, anger or grief;

there is still a real God up there who loves you
and (according to Psalm 139) thinks about you so
many times each day that you can't even count them.

And, in reality, there is a real God up there who
has a very special love for "widows and orphans." Any
person who is divorced or has a mate die is an emotional "widow." Any child whose parent died *or
divorced* is an emotional "orphan." Broken homes and
stepfamilies are people for whom God has a special
love and concern.

I would be the first to grant you your argument
that God frequently *doesn't* come through for you the
way *you* want Him to. If we had *our* way, God would
be always there to wave a magic wand and clear up all
of our difficulties *immediately* (if not sooner)!

Instead, God allows us to suffer consequences for
the mistakes we make, and sometimes even for the
mistakes made by others in our life. He allows us to
suffer, to seek relief, to look at options, to make decisions, to make mistakes, to forgive ourselves, to
regroup, to try again. In short, He allows us to mature
and learn how to cope and survive in this depraved
world through the college of "life's hard knocks." He
promises us that there is an eternal "happily ever after"
ending in the next life for all who trust Christ's death
on the cross and resurrection for the payment of their
sins. And He asks us to believe that He really does love
us and that He allows, in the long run, what is best for

our personal growth . . . in spite of the fact that His ways of doing things are not our ways!

If I were God, I would run things much differently! That's why He won't let me have His job!

As a psychiatrist, I know good and well that 90 percent of the suffering we go through is brought on by our own:

1. lack of proper emotional insights
2. lack of training
3. sinful errors
4. or innocent errors. Ten percent of the suffering we go through is probably unavoidable and necessary.

The purpose of this book is to reach out in love to the "widows" and "orphans" of this world, and their loved ones, and to those who also love these widows and orphans. Our goal is to help eliminate the 90 percent of their suffering that is unnecessary.

In the Old and New Testaments God inspired the human authors to write more than one hundred twenty passages of scripture on widows and orphans. God loves them. He wants people to love them, too. He wants the church to make their needs a *primary* ministry. He wants them to feel included and significant. He wants them to forgive and love themselves biblically. We live in a corrupt, prejudiced society. Even churches attempt to serve God in corrupt and prejudiced ways. Many churches and church leaders have been polluted by worldly philosophies and try vainly to measure their own spirituality by such stupid things as:

1. amount of offering
2. ability to pray long prayers or publicly

exhibit "spiritual gifts"

3. legalism

4. position of leadership in the church (power)

If you want to know how God measures true spirituality, just read scripture verses like James 1:26-27.

> If anyone considers himself religious and yet does not keep a tight rein on his tongue, he deceives himself and his religion is worthless. Religion that God our Father accepts as pure and faultless is this: to look after orphans and widows in their distress and to keep oneself from being polluted by the world.

May God bless the churches who provide father substitutes, who include and welcome the divorced, who reach out in creative ways to educate and counsel the widows and orphans in their communities. May God bless the "widows" who have made sinful past choices or who have suffered from the sinful choices of others. May God bless the widows who have suffered the death of a mate, or who have never married. And may God love and bless and provide for the needs of all sorts of orphans (by death, by divorce, or by the workaholism of a parent). May God use all of us to minister to these young sheep that the Good Shepherd so dearly loves.

Paul Meier, M.D.

CHAPTER TWO

The Storm After The Calm

Brewing Storms

Guidelines for a stepfamily? Is a stepfamily any different from a "regular" family? When divorced people with children remarry, they make a family just like everyone else, don't they? Everybody just works it out and fits into a new family. What could go wrong if two people really love each other and want to make a new family life together? These are some of the questions that unsuspecting people never think to ask. They really don't know that the calm is often over and the storm is brewing.

Case Study: Shake-and-Bake Family

For instance, Sue cried bitterly as she explained how her second marriage was crumbling before her eyes. There had been no major problems in their marriage. As well-paid professionals, both she and her husband lived safe and secure lives. Any quarrels were quickly and kindly resolved. In the first year-and-a-half of marriage, nothing went wrong. Then his children came to live with them and the storm after the calm hit.

Case Study: Yours, Mine, and Ours

Tom and Betty were married two years after each of them had been through emotionally draining divorces. Their courtship was like a movie script. Each had gained custody of their children through the divorce. After deciding upon the wedding date, they both believed that the storms in their lives were over and that they could start living again. Tom and Betty felt that their four elementary-aged children would blend nicely into a new family and be a "normal" family. Three years later they had a baby boy. Their joy soon vanished with the onset of problems in the "yours, mine and ours" family.

Case Study: Telling Them About Him/Her

In another family, fifteen-year-old Steve did not know what had happened. He had been an honor student and was active at his high school. He was on the football and track teams, earning the respect of both his coaches and teammates. Even Steve's home-room teacher had mentioned that he was in line for the school's service award. Life was going along great, even though his mother had divorced his father two years before. Then Steve's mother met Jake and married him after a quick and intense romance. The suddenness of the romance and marriage hit Steve harder than a linebacker. He really didn't like Jake and showed it in every way possible. Steve's mother was learning the hard way about telling her son about him.

Case Study: If I Had It To Do Over

"I just don't understand it." lamented 38-year-old Jim. "When we were dating, everything went so well. We never fought. I guess that is why we were married so quickly. After we were married, things really changed, and in a hurry. We disagreed about money, the kids, work, and friends. We got so angry with each other that we haven't even talked in a week. The kids are running wild and our life is a mess. How could I have made this mistake?" Jim, too, experienced the results of remarrying too hastily and found himself saying, "If only I had it to do over again."

Case Study: The Other Person in Our Lives
Soon after remarrying, Max discovered that his children were acting differently toward his new wife, Lynn. The children became sharp and disrespectful with her. This soon carried over into their relationship with him. His thirteen-year-old daughter began to defy him openly while his ten-year-old son threatened to go live with his real mom on a permanent basis. Tension increased in the home in snowballing proportions. Max couldn't understand the reasons for all of the hostility. Lynn treated the children better than their own mother. In desperation, he called his former wife and asked her for her support in the situation. She replied that if he couldn't handle the children he ought to give them to her fulltime. Max was beginning to learn some of the problems of the other person in our lives.

Case Study: The Summit Meeting
Not wanting to start an open confrontation Peggy discouraged her new husband Pete from being more assertive with her elementary-aged children. They were becoming a problem at home and in school. At home they wouldn't do their chores or participate in the normal matters of day-to-day living, while at school they were getting into academic and disciplinary problems. Peggy was unaware of a useful tool in stepparenting — the summit meeting.

Case Study: *Outside, Looking In*

As he sat in his living room for another lonely night, Paul wondered why his children refused to be with him. Four times in the last two weeks he had made plans to be with them, only to have them cancel out at the last minute. Each time a pain of loneliness shot through his body. Losing Millie through divorce was traumatic, but then to lose the children through their rejection of him severed his last remembrance of a warm family. The pain of being on the outside looking in was something Paul never thought he would experience.

Case Study: *Happy/Painful Days*

Opening the local section of the newspaper, Cheryl did not expect to see what she saw. There it was — a full-length story about her son and his recent winning of a large nationwide scholarship contest. The story also went on to tell of his athletic successes and immense popularity at the local high school. In the fall, he would be going to a prestigious college on both an academic and athletic scholarship. Tears of happiness mingled with tears of sorrow. Cheryl had not seen her son in over a year. She hadn't shared much of his life since she and her husband divorced. At best, these past few years of partial sharing in her son's life were happy/painful days for Cheryl.

Case Study: *The Bond that Isn't There*

After months of trying to be a father to his three stepchildren, Rudy was on the verge of stopping the efforts. No matter what he said or did, the children did not respond. He loved their mother deeply. He even loved the two teenaged boys and 10-year-old girl as his own, but they certainly didn't return the love. At times they treated him like a stranger. Troubled and depressed, Rudy went to a counselor to ask what he could do about the bond that isn't there.

It's not Really the Same

As in the preceding cases and with thousands more, "it's not really the same" becomes more evident. Intact families (natural parents and their children) are different from stepfamilies (one natural parent and one stepparent with various combinations of step and natural siblings). To assume that both families will be the same and develop in the same manner is in error. They're just not the same.

More Divorce and More Stepchildren

Each of the people in the preceding cases faced a source of major conflict in a remarriage situation. That conflict is now believed to be the leading cause of marital problems in a remarriage. The problem, ironically, is also one of the major reasons why many seek remarriage—children. Unfortunately, the problem is not lessening. In the mass of statistics that flow out of governmental agencies, the numbers concerning remarriages that involve children are staggering. Millions of Americans have been divorced. Since 1970 the rate has increased 80 percent. The average number of children who become involved in these divorces has increased 33 percent. In 1970, one of every eight children lived in a stepfamily setting, with at least one nonbiological parent. Some researchers estimate that there are currently fifteen million children living in stepfamily situations.

The facts, of course, are alarming. Yet Americans still desire to raise children in a family setting. And because of this desire, remarriages will continue to occur. More and more children will be raised in stepfamilies. Specifically, fifty percent of all those people who divorce have children and will remarry. Yet over half of these people will get a second divorce, usually within the first five years of a second marriage.

Obviously, the problems of marital decay in this nation lie in the basic avoidance of biblical principles for creating a growing marriage. Yet marriages do occur and children are raised in stepfamilies. Many concerned stepparents are thus asking, "What are some of the causes of the frictions? What can be done to smooth out the rough spots?"

Accepting Divorce Realities

Each of these questions is complex and does not just necessarily "go away" with time. Before an understanding of these problems is reached, two far more important issues must be understood.

The Responsibility of Remarrying

God's plan is not to resort to divorce as a "fire escape" or an easy way out. That certainly is not the impact of Jesus' words in Matthew 5:32-33: "And it was said, 'Whoever divorces his wife, let him give her a certificate of dismissal'" (NASB). The thrust of Scripture is to work out marital problems. Even in the case of an adulterous mate, Scripture indicates that forgiveness is still the key word, not divorce. Jesus said that forgiveness is an ongoing process. "Then Peter

20

came and said to Him, 'Lord, how often shall my brother sin against me and I forgive him? Up to seven times?' Jesus said to him, 'I do not say to you seven times, but up to seventy times seven' "(Matt. 18: 21,22, NASB). Yet divorce goes on and on, and in increasing numbers.

It is mandatory that those who are considering remarrying search their own hearts and the Scriptures before making that decision. This may, however, require the counsel of a friend, a pastor, or Christian professional who will help guide in this decision. Thus, the purpose of this book is to help those who have married again and find themselves in a stepfamily situation.

Although God promises forgiveness, the scars of sin may still remain. "If we confess our sins, He is faithful and righteous to forgive us our sins and to cleanse us from all unrighteousness" (1 John 1:9 NASB). David experienced the consequences of sin in losing his son. Moses felt the effects when he couldn't enter the Promised Land after striving for it for over forty years. Paul anguished over the aftermath of his sin through some of the thoughts he had. The first couple on the earth experienced the forgiveness of God, yet they still suffered the consequences. This is certainly not to condemn forever divorced people who marry again, since this is not God's attitude.

Accepting the Consequences

The point is that divorced people who marry again must be willing to accept and work with those special consequences that will come because they are divorced and remarried. This book will help to identify those special problems involving children. To play ostrich and "stick one's head in the sand" and pretend that things will just work out is to add new consequences onto the ones already existing. God is willing and able to help these new families gain the love, growth, and support that is so vital. Some problems will be there for life; they will never go away. The families may pray and pray, but still they may not go away. That may be a consequence that remains.

Feeling like a second-class citizen is not God's plan for any of His children. Divorced children of God are still just as important to Him. He loves them just as he loves all of the great Bible heroes. With this confidence, married-again people can move onto their special set of problems and experience God's working in them. It is not hopeless. Each problem that is experienced is an opportunity to see God's working. He may or may not change circumstances. This is important to understand.

God promises peace in circumstances; He does not promise to change circumstances. "Not that I speak from want; for I have learned to be content in whatever circumstance I am. I know how to get along with humble means, and I also know how to live in prosperity; in any and every circumstance I have learned the secret of being filled and going hungry, both of having abundance and suffering need. I can do all things through Him who strengthens me" (Phil. 4:11-13, NASB). God can certainly change circumstances; the Old Testament is rich with examples of how He changed circumstances. The guarantee is, that by yielding to the indwelling Holy Spirit every Christian has the power to be at peace in the bad circumstances (Eph. 5:18-20).

Stepfamilies and the Bible

One further word of encouragement before the adventure starts. Scripture has little to say on the current problem of stepfamilies. As a matter of fact, the word "stepchild" does not appear in the Bible. However, a look into the Bible does reveal that the situation did occur in varying instances. The first such case starts in Genesis 16 when Abraham fathered Ishmael by Hagar. The saga continued into Genesis 21 when Sarah became jealous of Abraham's "other son" and told him to get rid of the child. In Genesis 21:11 Scripture records that Abraham experienced much grief over this stepparenting encounter. Only God's comfort enabled him to handle the situation.

The Bible further reveals other similar "step situations." Eli raised Samuel as a son, even though the boy belonged to another. Moses was raised by Pharaoh's daughter and his natural mother. Consider David who had many children by many wives. Most people consider only Bathsheba as David's wife; but he did have several other wives with children by them. The palace must have been quite a war zone with stepchildren and stepmothers in every room. One has to wonder if David found the battlefield more peaceful than his own home.

Consider the Lord Jesus Christ and his earthly father. Would not Joseph be considered a stepfather by today's standards? Matthew records that Joseph did some soul-searching before God intervened and comforted him (Matt. 1:18-25). Imagine — the Lord

23

of the universe, the King of Kings, the Savior of man lived his earthly childhood and young adulthood with a stepfather! There must be hope! There must be joy in raising stepchildren. There must be an answer!

The analysis goes one more step. Jesus, in one of His countless confrontations with the Pharisees, advised them that they were of their father, the Devil. "You are of your father the devil, and you want to do the desires of your father. He was a murderer from the beginning, and does not stand in the truth, because there is no truth in him. Whenever he speaks a lie, he speaks from his own nature; for he is a liar, and the father of lies" (John 8:44, NASB). In not accepting Christ as Savior, they were, in effect, accepting Satan as their father. Then, all who do not accept Christ as Savior belong to the family headed by Satan. When a person accepts, by faith, Christ as his or her Savior from the penalty of sin, that person has eternal life guaranteed; and that person always changes families. He becomes God's child. "But as many as received Him, to them gave the right to become children of God, even to those who believe in His name" (John 1:12, NASB). In effect, believers become spiritual stepchildren! Just think about this. Everyone who has accepted Christ as Savior is really a stepchild. Certainly that is a refreshing way to start to learn to "grow in step."

CHAPTER THREE

It's Really Not The Same

New Family and New Differences

In a rush to get on with living, stepfamilies want to forget the past, patch everything together, and establish another family unit to carry on just as if nothing had ever happened. Soon, however, many families learn that things just aren't the same. In order to weather these differences, families must understand what the differences are and why. With this knowledge applied in the new family unit, it must be different, but the new structure need not be built on sand.

Americans want to live in a family unit. This unit provides security, serenity, structure, and support. Even with the unfortunate major trend to live together without being married, people are still revealing their basic need to belong to a family unit. What is unique about the family unit is that it "grows" through stages just as the person does. The family moves through predictable stages that are vital for the healthy development of its members, as well as of the family unit itself.

The Intact Family: Marriage to Empty Nest

Stages One and Two: Marriage and Children
An intact family moves through five definite stages. The first is the originating step of marriage.

Following marriage comes the birth of children — stage two. Stage three ih often the longest and sometimes most trying for the family — the individualization of family members. This stage deserves some explanation.

Stage Three: Separating into an Individual

For the first time that John says. "Please, I want to do it myself" to the time when Sue comes home early from a date and says, "Mom and Dad, I want you to meet somebody pretty special," children are becoming separate persons. This is often hard for parents to watch, even though they may welcome and want it. Children are learning that they are different from Mom and Dad and must assume responsibilities for their own destiny. The first child to leave home changes the roles of the children who are still at home. Suddenly, someone else becomes the new "oldest child at home."

The traumas that children develop, as they start to realize that parents are not an extension of themselves, are real. Yet, leaving an infant in the church nursery is one of the first necessary parts of the process. Sleeping alone in a room is another example of this healthy separation. When adolescence starts, children not only learn that they are different from their parents, but that they are different from others as well.

In order to complete successfully this transition into the outside world, the adolescent child often relies upon the home and family to be a security base in which to evaluate, recuperate, and launch out again. Hence, the adolescent becomes assuming and parents

26

may often feel that the child is using the home without taking any family responsibilities. Many battles are fought over this issue. In a stepfamily this aspect of separation may often be World War III.

Not to be left out are parents who are starting to detach themselves from the roles they played with their children in earlier years. No longer do the parents invest the quantity of time that they once did. Being needed by their children no longer means tying their shoestrings. Now it means giving them the keys to the car. Instead of playing ball with the child, parents now watch the child play with other children on an organized team. "Daddy, may I go with you?" is replaced by "Daddy, may I go with them?" Necessary, but painful, these changes help all of the family to become mature individuals.

Stage Four: Leaving the Nest

Returning to the stages of development, the fourth stage is the reality of the third stage. Actual departure of the children is the final culmination of the individualizing process. When the first child moves out, gets married, or goes to college, the family moves into another growth period and starts to adjust to their loss. The final resolution of this stage is full acceptance or adjustment to the loss. Since children come and go in this stage, it, too, is often prolonged. From weekend vacations from college to Sunday afternoon visits for dinner, this stage may be years in length.

Stage Five: Living with an Empty Nest

Since parents still want their children to need them and often want to continue directing their young-adult lives, struggles may develop. The children desire to feel and be independent, and yet they may still want the attention that they received at home. These opposite feelings can lead to conflicts and hurt feelings, but they can lead to both parties moving into the fifth and final stage. As parents and children begin adult communication about the differences they may have, they move into stage five, the integration of the loss.

A college senior returned home for the Thanksgiving holiday and noticed that his parents had remodeled the living and dining rooms and had even added the family's first color television. The son remarked, "Why didn't you guys do this when I was home, so that I could enjoy it?" The father calmly answered, "The reason we didn't do it was because you were home!" The son and parents then entered a time of life when the relationship moved to a new level of acceptance. Yes, they are still parent/son, but now they are all adults, living and functioning separately in the adult world.

Another family did not fare as well when, at various times, all of the adult children lived at home. Each would have an emotional conflict with one parent over a certain activity or action, move out in anger, and return a few weeks later to assume the role of a child once more. This serious pattern seemed almost adolescent. Upon further insight, it was seen that the adult-comprised family was still indeed acting in stage three — individualization of family members.

The Step Family: Recovery to Blending
As stated before, healthy families move through

these stages with varying degrees of difficulty. Small families may find more conflicts within the stages. Larger families often have fewer, since they have more examples to look at and to model after and less time to have conflicts. But stepfamilies are not the same. Their system is only three stages long.

Step One: Losing and Gaining Relationship

In stepfamilies, the first stage is recovering from the loss and entering into a new relationship. What losses do they have? Each suffers many individual as well as corporate losses. For example, each child loses the family unit, the physical presence of one parent, and the possible loss of a lifelong home and neighborhood. Financial insecurity, possible alienation from a group of relatives, and even the chance of the loss of a sibling may compound the recovery further. The losses for the parents are similar and equally painful. The extent and degree of these losses often makes the second half of the stage — entering into new relationships — even more difficult.

The extent of the losses may divert so much of the child's emotional energy just to coping that little is left over for developing mandatory or optional new relationships. Mandatory new relationships include those with natural parents. One now is removed and often is unavailable, while the other now acts as both parents. Each child also must move into a new position within the family. Each may not have the freedom to be a child any longer and must assume certain new duties because "we now all have to pitch in together." If the mother has custody and must leave the home to work, then, in effect, the child loses both parents through the divorce. The child may be hard pressed to see how anyone else can be suffering more than he or she. Acting-out behavior, emotional changes, or poor school performance may indicate that these feelings indeed are being experienced by the child.

Step Two: Accepting Another Family

This first stage may last for a few months, a few years, or a lifetime. However, if the custodial parent starts to date again and a relationship becomes serious, the second stage begins. As the parent is trying to conceptualize and visualize another marriage, so too is the child. The child may visualize losing the parent all over again. Acquiring a stepparent often causes a child to feel as if he or she is betraying a removed natural parent. Finally, the child may conceptualize giving up the attention that, even now, must be shared. Explaining or telling children about the seriousness of the relationship and/or future marital plans is not something to be taken lightly, as will be explained later.

In many cases, these first two stages may occur simultaneously and in a short period of time. In contrast, the stages of the intact family, which are tied into the emotional development of the children, may take several years to complete. At a time when children are progressing through some sensitive and emotional stages, a parent contemplating a second marriage is often moving very quickly and without a great deal of sensitivity toward the children. Thus, a stepfamily forces children to speed up changes that they would normally make over a longer period of time and in a more secure setting. For example, a special need of adolescents is the stability of the home to help them move safely through the teen years. Because of this, the potential for volatile family conflicts is probable when the stepfamily is new, insecure, and unsolidified.

Step Three: Blending Together
The last stage of a stepfamily is the process of reconstitution, or blending together. Just as our nation's founders took a great deal of time and experienced considerable conflict in producing a constitution which has lasted for almost two hundred years, the stepfamily may take years to "reconstitute" and get on with living. With two newly remarried people desiring to forget the pain of the past in the tranquility of a new home and family, patience is often not a major characteristic. The excitement and newness of being married again is a powerful attraction for the new husband and wife, which is understandable, but often not to children.

In following chapters, the vital aspects of how to negotiate this "reconstitution" will be addressed. With the understanding that reconstituted families are unique, stepparents will be able to see matters of discipline, living standards, relationships, removed natural parents, and stepsiblings in their proper context. They may also see these factors vary with the age of the children.

When It Hurts The Most

Toddlers and Elementary Age
Not only are stages of family development different for the stepfamily, but the effects may be different on the children according to their age level.

For example, elementary-aged children may be extremely expressive over the loss of the removed parent. Consequently, their grieving may result in some regressive behavior or even gross misbehavior. Such actions as bed-wetting, thumb-sucking, or poor school adjustment may occur. To say that this greatly affects the guilt of the remaining parent is an understatement. Yet, children must go through their own grieving processes, and their behaviors may indicate this. Vital to the grieving process is the custodial parent's willingness to discuss with the child the missing natural parent. Not to allow the child to express his or her anger, guilt, or loneliness is to stagnate the child's healing.

It is difficult to discuss someone who may have been a marital partner, but children do not understand this. In reality, they shouldn't be expected to do so. A parent's reluctance to talk about an absent parent with a child may produce some unwanted emotions in the child. It may produce the desire to be with the missing parent even more. The child may even instigate conflicts to get the parents together (since it can't be done normally). In its true meaning, the message to the child is, "It's not okay to talk about Mom or Dad, so I'm going to find out why." That attitude often leads to some unhealthy behaviors.

Pre-teens

For the pre-adolescent, the effects become more complex. While working out his or her own identity, the pre-adolescent may not realize how much the divorce has disrupted his or her life. Therefore, the child in this age bracket may blame either parent for the divorce and all the pain it has produced. The intensity of these feelings can leave the pre-teen in a lonely or passive state. Feelings of worry and despair may accompany this grieving process.

Because of their emerging personalities, pre-teens sense a never-before-felt need for fairness. As they are entering the adult world, it is now most important for them to be treated fairly. Consequently, they become judges of others' "fair" and "unfair" acts. In a divorce, it is extremely difficult for them not to make these critical judgments and to act them out accordingly. For the pre-teen, aligning with the "wronged parent" is a common manner of resolving these apparent inequities.

Acting-out behavior is the most apparent indication of the pre-teen's struggle over the divorce. Suppressed emotions are expressed in outward, symbolic actions. A need for attention from a missing parent may manifest itself in cruelty to the present parent. Feelings of being misunderstood and frustration can erupt with physical abuse of siblings. Resentment of a new stepparent authority may be seen in a sudden resentment of all authority, including school. Even a drop in school and/or athletic performance can indicate a struggling over this divorce.

Two guidelines become critical in understanding pre-teens in a divorced or stepfamily. If a pre-teen exhibits a new and sudden inappropriate behavior without an apparent and reasonable cause, the child may be acting out behavior stemming from emotional needs concerning the divorce and/or stepfamily.

Second, the inappropriate behavior must be disciplined whether or not the feelings are disciplined. By this time, however, spanking only inflames the problem. Relating discipline to the offense often works wonders, since it teaches the pre-teen that inappropriate behaviors have consequences. Customary consequences are often imposing restrictions and removing privileges.

However, the pre-teen must be taught, then given the opportunity, for proper expression of those inner feelings. If this involves spending additional time with the removed parent, then this must be done! If it means that the present natural parent needs to deal with some uncomfortable issues, then this must be done! Not to do this is to treat only the symptoms.

A final consideration of the pre-teen is that physical symptoms are common manifestations of his or her inward anxieties. Many household chores have fallen victim to a pre-teen's sudden pretense of a headache or upset stomach. To the dismay of the parent, as soon as the chore is completed by someone else, the pre-teen miraculously regains health and bolts out the front door to join friends in some activity. "Had again!" is the feeling of the "taken" parent. Similar physical problems may occur when the pre-teen deals with the "unfair" removal of a parent.

This is classic passive-aggressive behavior, so characteristic of the pre-teen. To over-react to an inwardly-grieving pre-teen only drives deeper wedges between parent and child. Instead, giving restrictions and removing privileges not only creates an atmosphere of emotional openness but also produces change.

Teens
Full adolescence is a time of great change and

excitement. Children are moving daily into maturity. Parents enjoy even more the accomplishments and successes of their children. Many even become deep friends during this period. When this normal transition time to adulthood is interrupted, adolescents may resolve the tensions in devastating ways. Again, acting out behavior is common. Since teenagers may act out repressed feelings in active rather than passive behavior, they may resort to more disruptive acts. Staying away from home, for example, may be the manner in which an adolescent expresses his or her anger over parents disrupting the home. Parent loss can be a major fear of an adolescent. One way in which he or she copes with these feelings is to stay away from the constant reminder.

As an adolescent emerges sexually, the awareness of sexual interest is keen. Struggling with one's own sexuality may be traumatic, but often this struggle becomes a crisis when a parent starts to date someone else. Some adolescents may feel that the dating parent is being immature, unfair, or not leaving time for helping them through their own sexual struggles. Consequently, they may seek sexual comfort through premarital sex.

Losing a parent forces an adolescent to see that he or she is still dependent on that parent. Admitting this is something the teen tries to avoid. To resolve this still active dependency, the teen may become dependent not only on sexual relationships, but also alcohol, drugs, peer groups, or substitute parents. Again, treating the inappropriate behavior with an atmosphere of emotional openness is vital.

From the different stages of stepfamily development to the various manners in which various-aged children handle divorce, all factors point to one conclusion. The stepfamily is not the same as the intact family. With this in mind, different strategies must be developed and implemented to facilitate this transition and growth. Even though God has not put a specific book in the Bible to guide stepparents, His Word is exhaustive. It gives those who desire instruction the wisdom to avoid the "storm after the calm" and to "grow in step."

CHAPTER FOUR

If I Had It To Do Over, I Would . . .

Why People Remarry

Prayerfully, Christians take great care in selecting their mates. The Lord admonishes every Christian, "Unless the Lord builds the house, They labor in vain who build it . . ."(Psalm 127:1a) and "Do not be bound together with unbelievers . . ."(2 Cor. 6:14a). Often, this initial marital decision is made with much flair, romance, and time.

In a remarriage, the decisions often are hurried and not prayerfully considered. This happens not only because of the person's lack of spiritual insight, but because of his psychological nature, as well. Somehow, people forget to read the "fine print" in the marital contract. More correctly, they do not really take the time to see what that fine print really is.

Even before considering a possible remarriage, each person needs to come to understand his or her "fine print" reasons for marrying. Unless the foundation of the remarriage is solid, it is only a matter of time before this marriage too will come apart, regardless of any stepfamily problems. What are some of the more common "fine print" reasons why people remarry?

The White Knight

In haste to get out of a marriage, people may focus only on their former mate and the pain involved in that relationship. Often they do not take time to understand how the divorce will greatly alter their lives. Suddenly, a husband is responsible for feeding himself, cleaning his house, and doing his own laundry. If he survives this, he must then battle the lines at the grocery store, figure out whom he can get to sew on a button, and develop a system for remembering his parents' and childrens' birthdays. That isn't all, for soon the reality of budget-straining child-support payments sets in. He realizes that he can only afford a small, one-bedroom apartment and must give up vacations.

Wives are affected, as well. In traditional cultures, a wife is usually not adept at home and car repairs. If she is not knowledgable, how can she know if the repairman is really being honest? Does it need to be fixed? Further complicating this problem is that most divorced women with children suffer greater financial hardships than divorced husbands. In a few years, the husband may regain some financial stability, while the wife may not do so for years to come.

In either case, both may be looking for the "white knight" to come riding into their lives on a silver stallion to relieve the situation. The greater the desire for someone to do this, the greater the possibility of a shaky base to a second marriage. Sooner or later, somebody may tire of being the rescuer and will want to stop. In this case, marital heroes fall hard and quick and with even greater emotional trauma than in a first marriage. Both people must understand what the other expects in these areas before they "sign the contract." If not, "white knights" become tarnished pawns.

Hear No Evil, See No Evil
The emotional destructiveness of a divorce is massive. It is often so much so that some people choose never to discuss it again. Avoiding this necessary soul-searching is another reason why some people are attracted to a potentially harmful second marriage. They may feel comfortable with someone because that person does not press or ask about previous marital problems.

Such was the case for Darren. His first marriage was a heart-breaking and emasculating process. His deep sensitivity about failure and inability to make the marriage work ran deeply in his emotional life. Those emotions kept him from opening up in several dating relationships following the divorce. As his relationships started to progress and deepen, Darren avoided all mention of his first marriage. Feeling that the divorce had rendered him unfit and incompetent, he concluded that opening up to another woman would only leave him vulnerable again to those pains. This is why he was attracted to Terri so quickly.

Terri never pressed him about his first marriage, believing that, after they were married, he would open up and trust her. Darren saw Terri's non-threatening communication as "ideal." He would be able to hide his inner feelings and never tell anyone. Consequently, their dating life was active, carefree, fun, and superficial. Friends from their singles' class at church encouraged them, since they seemed to be the "ideal couple," and so they were married. After six months, Terri concluded that Darren should be secure enough in their marriage now to move into a deeper relationship. However, the more Terri begged Darren to share inner thoughts, the more evasive he became. He retorted with sharp, critical remarks about her and started staying longer at the office. He became increasingly distant. Terri and Darren had not realized the importance of being emotionally open before marriage. Openness before marriage sets the stage for it during marriage.

He/She is Good with the Kids

Parenting is not an easy job. Parenting is a joyous job. What a paradox this is! While children certainly are a "gift of the Lord" (Psalm 127:3a), at times they are certainly . . . well, a challenge! This paradox is often intensified with a single parent. Intact families have two parents to help each other, whereas a single parent has no one. Feeling the stress of raising the children alone and the guilt over breaking up their home, some divorced parents often look for another parent instead of another mate. They may express this directly to the other person. Often it is just assumed that the new mate will take over the role and everything will become the "little white cottage with the white picket fence."

Jan had divorced her husband when Todd was two years old. She had tried to hold the marriage together, but her husband became involved in one affair after another. His drinking had become such a problem that he lost several jobs. Finally, when he left her, she obtained a divorce. The next few years were traumatic. She had only Todd for emotional support, and a toddler is not the most supportive person in the world. At the park or at church, Todd would follow some of the men around and crave the slightest attention.

40

A few years after her divorce, Jan met another man who not only liked her, but Todd also. Jan carefully did not push the relationship with Todd so that Andy would not be frightened off. After all, he was really good with Todd, and that was important. Within a year they were married but the next years were filled with anxiety and frustration. Jan tried to force a relationship between Todd and Andy. After several years of this tension, their marriage deteriorated to the brink of divorce. Jan had put her desire for a father for Todd ahead of the choice of a husband. The selection of a second mate is no less important that the first in achieving a "forever" marriage.

After Him/Her, Anyone Looks Good

As a teenager, Angela had always wanted her marriage to be just like the movies, and things started out on course. She had a high school sweetheart. She worked while he went to college. They married soon after his graduation, had three children, attended a nice church, and enjoyed a comfortable life. Soon, however, it all became a mess. Sam changed. Did he ever change! After getting a job with a large corporation, he quickly moved up the ladder, reaching top management by age thrity-two. Then the change came.

First Sam started to buy expensive toys — boats and cars. His work-associated travel suddenly started to increase, taking him to rather exotic places. Their once active sexual life began to dwindle, yet Sam did not complain. The children noticed that Daddy was different. He didn't come to their games and recitals anymore, always with the excuse that he had to work. The Sunday school class, once a source of fellowship and activity to him, was now dull and boring. Angela kept defending Sam to the children and friends. She reasoned that he was under much pressure and that they would all have to sacrifice for a year or so, but when Sam got things leveled out, then everything would be back to normal.

However, the dream turned into a nightmare. It started as Angela and the children were returning from church family night. Knowing the children were disappointed that their dad had not been with them, Angela decided to surprise Sam and stop by the office. As she drove by, she saw that Sam's car was not there. The office building was completely dark and locked. Puzzled, she pulled out of the parking lot and started toward home. As she did, a small red sports car with a blond-haired woman driving pulled into the lot. Sam was in the car!

Holding back the tears, Angela drove home. Her imagination was running wild, while her emotions were still trying to rationalize. She waited for Sam and confronted him with what she had seen. Instead of answering her, he confessed to her that he was in legal trouble. He had been involved in some illegal contract work and was being investigated.

As the evening continued, more of the sordid details came out. The blond was not the first affair; there had been many over the last few years. Sam had used all of their savings to finance so-called "business trips," which were weekend affairs with a series of girls. Angela tried to handle it by asking the Lord to help her forgive him, but when Sam said that he hadn't loved her for years and wanted out, she was crushed.

The next few months were painful, as more and

more of Sam's extra-marital affairs came out. He had taken a second mortgage on the house and spent it on some questionable investments. Within a few months Angela lost her financial security, her home, and her husband — her high school sweetheart!

In her post-divorce life, Angela struggled with anger, fear, and worry. She seemed to lose her spirit and zest for living. She became involved with two men who also were struggling with life. Both times, Angela fell in love quickly but each relationship ended painfully. She had lost sense of discretion because, as she said, "After Sam, anyone looks good."

In choosing a second mate, comparing the new mate with the former only prolongs pain and agony and leaves one open to repeat past mistakes. A Christian should compare a new mate with Biblical guidelines, not with weaknesses of a former spouse, then a new mate can be chosen with the expressed standards that God has for mates. This comparison leads to healthy choices.

It All Seemed So Right

Tim had just won a year-long custody hearing and received residential custody of the children. The divorce had taken over one year from start to finish. The marriage had been in trouble for several years prior to that time, but Tim had wanted to stay together for the sake of the children. However, that didn't happen, and what had involved many years ended in a few minutes. The judge ruled and those years of marriage were swept into history. Tim was alone and a single parent.

Tim met Lisa at church in the singles' class. They

really hit it off well. She had just come out of a brutal divorce and was feeling many of the same things that Tim was feeling. They spent countless hours sharing and relating how these divorces had devastated them. Raising children as a single parent monopolized many of their early discussions. They started to develop a bond that stemmed from being caught up in the same situation. In developing a dependency on one another, they felt that no one else would really understand their situation. Each discussion led to further closeness and more dependencies. The intensity and similarities of their circumstances became a great attraction.

Throughout their courtship, Tim and Lisa analyzed, discussed, and produced many good thoughts and ideas about their divorces and the problems of being alone after so many years of marriage. Yet, because of the intensity of the situation, neither one wanted to take deeper emotional risks. Both assumed that the essentials of marriage would work out, since they had become so compatible. Tim and Lisa allowed the intensity of their common feelings to cloud rational, spiritual direction in seeking a second marriage. After the wedding they experienced further pain which neither ever expected.

Emotionally, divorced single parents can often be swept away when meeting someone who has gone through a similar experience. This leads to the assumption that if the person is so understanding in one area, then he/she will be the same in all other areas. What is not seen is that the discussions and late-night talks are usually about one or two issues. Avoidance of important marital issues is not a solid foundation for considering compatibility. God admonishes couples to dwell in complete understanding and knowledge of each other:

> *Wives, in the same way be submissive to your husbands so that, if any of them do not believe the word, they may be won over without talk by the behavior of their wives, when they see the purity and reverence of your lives. Your beauty should not come from outward adornment, such as braided hair and the wearing of gold jewelry and fine clothes. Instead, it should be that of your inner self, the unfading beauty of a gentle and quiet spirit, which is of great worth in God's sight. For this is the way the holy women of the past who put their hope in God used to make themselves beautiful. They were submissive to their own husbands, like Sarah, who obeyed Abraham and called him her master. You are her daughters if you do what is right and do not give way to fear. Husbands, in the same way be considerate as you live with your wives, and treat them with respect as the weaker partner and as heirs with you of the gracious gift of life, so that nothing will hinder your prayers.*
>
> *1 Peter 3:1-7*

This can only happen when couples make it happen.

I Want Out Of The Singles' Class
Nan had been divorced for four years and was doing

well. She had received some money from the divorce settlement and had purchased a modest townhouse in a good neighborhood. Her son seemed to be happy with the situation and not overly concerned about not having a father in the home. Her job was a good one and she had received two promotions since the divorce.

Nan was active socially. Church activities, clubs, friends, and even a few nights at the spa filled her life. However, she felt life was passing her by. Her son provided emotional stimulation, especially since he was doing well in school and in sports, but something was missing. The singles' class had been great during the first two years. It warmed up those otherwise cold, lonely nights. The people were fun and supportive. However, now the class just wasn't the same. She found herself not really wanting to go home, even though her son was there. Then she met Ed.

Carefully guarding herself against involvement, Nan limited her time with Ed. Their romance was not really a romance; it seemed that she just felt comfortable with him. Some things bothered her about Ed, but she really didn't want to bring them up, since her life was beginning to have some excitement. Soon she realized that Ed was very serious about her, but that she didn't feel the same way. He wasn't a bad man and surely filled in the lonely times, she thought. After all, it was a way out of the singles' class and this lonely life.

Just as Nan felt the sting of adult loneliness, and at an early age, others likewise feel trapped in the same way. Often, these people will become involved with the very first person who seems interested. Mistaking removal of loneliness for marital love, they may marry into another stressful relationship.

Christians may be lonely, but they are never alone. Jesus promised, "I am with you always, even to the end of the age" (Matt. 28:20b). With this knowledge of Christ's promise, single parents need to see that there is a better option than marrying out of loneliness. It only requires waiting upon God's timing.

Choosing a Mate — Again!

Guideline One: A Mask of Self-deception
Is there a Biblical way to approach picking a second mate after the emotional and spiritual trauma of a marital breakup? Often, people will say that they "need a mate." This may lead to some serious error in choosing another one, since a Christian "needs" only Christ. The accurate statement of this emotion is that the person "wants" a mate. If one succumbs to the self-deception that he/she needs a mate, then the emotional focus may be upon finding someone, not upon asking God to lead. If a person has unhealthy and unrecognized dependency needs, he/she may be attracted to someone who apparently fills these dependencies, not to someone who will make a spiritually and emotionally healthy mate.

Guideline Two: Haste Makes Waste
Another guideline is to be cautious with someone who is in a hurry to get down the aisle. Paul warned Timothy to test men first before putting them into leadership positions (1 Tim. 3:10). This principle is crucial in a second marriage. Haste in a second marriage may only hasten a host of problems.

Guideline Three: Pre-marital Counseling — Again
Vital to the success of a second marriage is the use of sound counsel. "He who regards reproof is prudent" (Prov. 15:5b). Often a person's willingness to go through a pre-marital counseling period will give good indication of that person's emotional and spiritual stability. Reluctance to do this necessary healing and training function is a red-light warning that something is not right. A defensive attitude about a past marriage or reluctance to discuss current conflicts is not a healthy indicator that the person is ready for another marriage.

Guideline Four: Marry a Believer
Finally, Christians often get into a second marriage with an unbeliever. Because of many of the reasons previously mentioned, Christians will plunge headlong into a relationship with someone who is, at best, neutral about Jesus Christ. To be unequally yoked with unbelievers is often a prescription for emotional, physical, and spiritual turmoil. Before considering marrying another mate who will also become a stepparent, believers are wise to be aware of their psychological and emotional reasons for marrying. Because this new family is not like an intact family, the presures that will come will require two emotionally and spiritually mature people to function as a team. Without this maturity, growing in step will not occur.

CHAPTER FIVE

Telling Them About Him/Her

Happy Beginnings/Sad Endings

Case One: Maggie's Surprise

Maggie was crying as she sat in the counselor's office describing her mom's new boyfriend. She said that Mom had dated several men after divorcing Dad a year ago. But this time Maggie felt betrayed and hurt. Her mom had said, a few months ago, that she was going out with Bill, a man from work. They continued to date more and more. Bill even spent the evenings at the house, eating dinner and watching TV. He sometimes helped Maggie with algebra, "the curse of every ninth grader," according to Maggie. But Mom never said anything about the relationship. Maggie never even saw them embrace one another. She had thought there was nothing to worry about.

Case Two: Karen's Fights

Todd was eight and Mike was five. Karen had been divorced for almost two years, but really hadn't dated. She had tried, but the scene at the front door was traumatic every time a man would come to pick her up. The boys would cry, expecially Mike. Todd would whimper and lie on the floor with the look of impending death on his face. Once Mike even hit one of Karen's dates.

Case Three: The Honeymoon Is Over

Joan just couldn't believe that it was happening to them. All through their dating, she and Karl had been very careful to spend time with the four children, especially the two teens, Jason and Janna. Karl would come over every Sunday to take the whole family to church and they would all go out for Sunday dinner. Karl and Joan attended Jason's games and never missed one of Janna's concerts. The two little children seemed to "roll with the punches." Everything seemed right after a year of dating. So when Karl and Joan announced to the children that they were getting married, everyone seemed overjoyed.

The wedding was small but meaningful. Karl and Joan wanted to honor the Lord even through the ceremony. Janna sang, Jason was the best man, and the two little ones were ring bearers. In their public dedication, Karl and Joan declared their intention to honor the Lord in their marriage and family life.

Shortly after the honeymoon, things started to change. Jason became moody and removed. His grades began to drop and he was even benched by the coach. As the stresses mounted, Jason wanted to spend more time with his natural father who had not shown any interest in Jason for several years. It finally culminated one day when, after an argument over curfew, Jason demanded to go live with his father. Karl took it extremely hard and felt defeated and rejected, while Joan felt just helpless.

Janna was having similar difficulties. She started to skip her household duties and was picking on the two little ones more and more. She was sarcastic and rude to Karl, who didn't know how to handle the problem. Janna met some new friends, not from the church group, who were into some questionable activities. She began to lie and be less than honest as to where she spent her time. Seemingly overnight, Janna started to use "Well, all my friends are going" as justification for attending a questionable activity. Karl and Joan were perplexed. They didn't know what to do or where to turn.

Helping Children Through Divorce

These situations are often common or at least frequent in a stepfamily. As mentioned earlier, children go through a grief process over the loss of a parent in a divorce. Consequently, when the remaining parent starts to date, the grief process magnifies. Defining a time frame to begin dating is an individual matter, but some guidelines can be offered to help.

Guideline One: Resolve Divorce Questions

First, the now single parent must resolve the divorce spiritually and emotionally. This is critical, because children will need the remaining parent to help resolve their own conflicts. Of course, the removed parent can be involved as well, but lack of proximity may hinder this. Thus, when a child comes to a parent and says, "Did God want you to get divorced?" or, "If you want to do some fun things with an adult, why don't you call Daddy?" that parent must give the child an answer that heals, not "puts off." If the child hears a defensive and evasive answer, he or she may become angry, confused, or sad. Resolving spiritual and emotional matters is the first requirement for a parent before dating starts. With many, this process takes a year or more and often requires the help of a close friend, a pastor, or a professional counselor.

This may seem somewhat strict, but research supports that the greater the time period between the first and second marriage, the greater the success rate. Yes, the Lord is greater than statistics. There are exceptions to the research findings, but those exceptions are rare. During this interim time, single parents can fill the need for adult companionship by attending singles classes at church or social groups designed for people in the single-again life-style. Being either hasty or careless in choosing a second mate can be a guarantee that a second mistake is imminent. An extra year or so is a wise investment for the rest of one's life.

Guideline Two: Reassure Parenthood

During this time, the remaining parent as well as the removed parent can spend time with the children to reassure them that Mommy is still Mommy and Daddy is still Daddy. Give the children the opportunity to work through, ask about, and express unashamedly any feeling over the loss of the home and parents. This will take time, time, and more time. Remembering that the intact family is different from the stepfamily and from a transition family (between marriages), parents can help their children heal and grow if they will use this time to talk openly and frankly about the marriage, the divorce, and the future.

Guideline Three: Allow Understanding of the Loss

Since the loss of a parent is crunched into a

matter of months instead of several years, step children will need intense times of emotional resolution to help facilitate this transition. Also, each parent should prepare then for the questions that may follow and help the child understand and cope. One such question is often, "Does this mean that you may marry another man (or woman)?" For smaller children, the question may be worded, "Will you marry another Daddy (or Mommy)?" In either case, the child is trying to cope with the idea that another parent may one day come into his or her life.

Guideline Four: Recognize Unresolved Grief

Just as these questions indicate that the child is coping or, at least, starting the healing process, another question may indicate that it is not happening. A child who asks if the parent would ever remarry Mommy or Daddy may be indicating denial of the event or an inward fantasy (that may persist) of reuniting the two parents. If this continues for over a year, professional assistance may be necessary to help the child and the remaining family start the healing process. Whether he or she feels guilt or responsibility in the divorce or genuinely desires the reestablishment of the family, this denial by the child is not helping him or her to move on emotionally. Therefore, a parent would be wise in waiting until this stage is completed before dating.

Guideline Five: Discipline Biblically

God's Word offers some principles for newly-divorced parents to encourage them in this delicate matter. Proverbs 29:15 advises: "The rod of correction imparts wisdom, but a child left to itself disgraces his mother." This verse instructs that combining physical and verbal discipline brings wisdom to a child. Merely to punish a child because of acting-out behavior, anger changes in work or school habits, or other manifestations of a child's inability to cope with the divorce, does not bring wisdom or insight to the child or parent. As with any good parental discipline, physical punishment must be accompanied by verbal explanation or discussion of what has happened and why.

The second half of the verse lends even greater insight to the matter. A child who is left to his own devices or is undisciplined will bring his mother to shame. The verse seems to connote a mother who indulges a child. The child is one who is unrestrained or, in this case, left to resolve emotional hurts and concerns by himself. Previous illustrations have indicated how a child may bring shame to a mother. But what is the reason why parents, or mothers in particular, may indulge their child or children?

In many cases, guilt is the motivating factor. Guilt over breaking up the family, removing the children's father, bringing on financial hardships, and adding grief to childhood prompt many mothers not to confront or discipline their children. Even more, mothers may be unable to handle the guilt of the divorce or unable to help their children resolve it, so they do nothing about it. They only hope that the child will adjust on his or her own and somehow get through it. Often, the mother realizes too late that this is not going to happen and experiences the shame of

Proverbs 29:15. Mothers **must** talk to their children and discipline them in matters regarding the losses that occur through a divorce.

Scripture is not silent for fathers either. Ephesians 6:4 commands: "And fathers, do not provoke your children to anger; but bring them up in the discipline and instruction of the Lord." Fathers who are not willing to help their children work through a divorce may indeed provoke anger in their children. If the father is the removed parent, he may come to visit the children on weekends. Out of loneliness and/or guilt, he may want only to concentrate on making the weekend a fun and happy time, refusing to help the children work through the same emotional conflicts that they have with Mom at home. Again, fathers need to take time to help their children work through these conflicts. If a father complicates this with another dating relationship, he is stretched between two relationships which can work against one another. This avoidance strategy often merely delays a future conflict.

Preparing Children for Dating

Guideline One: Limit Exposure

After the critical first year has passed and a parent has started to date, several considerations must be made. If the children have resolved the loss of the other parent, they may now be looking at each new date as a potential stepparent or as competition for the remaining parent's affection. Thus, when a parent starts casual dating, he or she may want to limit the times that the date and the children are together. A sudden barrage of a new person may instill fears, hopes, or threats that really aren't valid, since a child or even an a adolescent may look at each date as Mom's or Dad's new steady boyfriend or girlfriend.

Guideline Two: Limit Family Dates
The parent also should not involve a dating relationship in stereotypic family settings or, at least, these should be limited. For if the new person gets involved quickly in emotional family settings, children may either fear the relationship or become overly attracted to the new person. If the relationship breaks off, then they have another loss to absorb. This is especially true for toddlers and preschool children.

Guideline Three: Keep Children Informed
When a child wants to know where Mom or Dad is going, it is best to answer the question. There is no need to go into a long dissertation on the merits of the person whom they are dating or why they want to attend a particular activity. A parent needs only to answer the questions directly. "I am going to a concert at church with a friend named Jim," or "I am going to dinner with a friend named Helen." This will help children start to accept the fact that Mom or Dad is developing new friends of the opposite sex and is doing social things with them. The wise parent, however, will not forsake their children by failing to do social things with them, also.

Guideline Four: Keep Children Aware
As a relationship continues, children have the right to know how it is progressing. In our enlightened

age children are much more aware of love and romance than those of previous generations. Not to be up front with them is to lay seeds of mistrust and doubt. So, keep them informed. A parent may say, "Honey, I really enjoy spending time with Bill (or Sue) and we really like each other. I love you though, and nothing will ever change that. Even if I am with Bill (or Sue), I want you to know that you are very special to me and that I always will be your Mom (or Dad) and will never leave you." As a child gets older, we change the words to fit the age, but the thought and idea are still the same. No other person will change our relationship with our children.

Guideline Five: Teens Need More

For the adolescent, some additional information may be needed. They may want to know why a parent has to date and go out. Early in the dating period, the parent may tell the adolescent that needs are different. Even though a parent's needs are different from an adolescent's, that should not change a parent/child relationship. This will be critical if a dating relationship moves into marriage. Words, however, need to be followed with actions, and especially with the adolescent who has the tendency to test words of adults to see if they really mean them. A dating parent is wise to show the adolescent that their relationship is stable. Tell them what is going on in a relationship. Spend time with the adolescent doing the things that the adolescent enjoys. Take time just to listen to the roller-coaster emotional responses of an adolescent.

Guideline Six: Move Slowly

Including the new person should be done slowly and systematically. Dinners at the house, games in the family room, and other non-threatening, light-hearted activities are good door openers. As the activities start to move out of the house and the dating relationship deepens, it is important that the new person in the family be active and directive. For example, Mom should not be the one who says, "Bill wants to take us to the zoo." Bill is the one who should say, "Hey, let's all go to the zoo on Saturday and then have a picnic." In doing this, Bill is setting a precedent to take leadership in a new home. Rather than doing this first in a disciplinarian context, he is doing it in a fun, hard-to-turn-down context. This pattern helps to facilitate a transition into a stepfamily. The same concept may be used for a prospective stepmother. Thus, the children may not feel that Mom or Dad is trying to force somebody upon them. In a sense, they are given the opportunity to accept or reject the new person.

Guideline Seven: Tell Children First

Keeping the children informed of the progression of the relationship makes the actual "announcement" somewhat less traumatic, as was discussed earlier in the case of Maggie. After careful prayer and seeking the advice of trusted Christian friends, the couple needs to inform the children immediately. Being careful not to let the announcement seem one-sided, both the natural and the potential stepparent should share equally in the announcement.

For example, Mom may say, "Bill and I have been praying and believe that our relationship has grown to the point that we want to be together for the rest of our lives." Bill may then add something like this: "Yes and your Mother and I want to be married so that we may have the opportunity to be together as man and wife and make us a new and special family." At this point, it is imperative that both reassure the children that they are not going to lose their special relationship with either one of the removed natural parents. By explaining and reassuring this fact over the life of the engagement period and on into the marriage, children may not feel the intense fear of losing a natural parent to a new mate.

Guideline Eight: Encourage Openness

After announcing the intentions to the children, both "parents" then may offer to let the children have time to think it over, so that they can all get together again and share any fears or apprehensions that anyone may have. This open and vulnerable time may not be easy for either the natural or stepparent, but it opens the doors to communications that will be vital in the coming years. Thus, with this as a foundation, both "parents" can be aware of the children's thinking and any change in attitudes up to and following the wedding.

When a new stepfamily includes natural children of both new mates, then an even different family structure is created. Their problems may be more complex. This special unit is discussed in Chapter Six, "Yours, Mine and Ours."

Taking "caring" time in telling the children about the new stepparent nurtures the new family to "grow in step."

Yours, Mine, And Ours

The New Brady Bunch

A few years ago it seemed so nice, such a wonderful thing to do. But it really didn't happen too often. About the only example that people could cite was the *Brady Bunch* television show. In that show, two single parents married and the story line portrayed their funny family exploits. Often the parents would arrive toward the end of the show and heal everything that the children had caused. Each episode ended with everything happy and back together again in familial bliss.

Holly and Don Get Canceled

Holly and Don met at a church-sponsored, single parents club. Holly had Jim, six, and Melissa, eight, while Don had custody of his two girls, Betty, seven, and Jamie, nine. Holly remembered spending hours with Don at the club discussing the struggles of raising the children and how to get by on her secretary's salary. Coping with the domestic side of raising two girls had been the emphasis of Don's discussions with Holly. They both seemed to help each other so much. Don came over to the house and fixed Holly's nagging house repairs. She returned the favors by spending time with the girls and helping them with many of their "growing pains."

Both felt that the other was an answer to prayer,

since neither of the children's other natural parents really wanted them. As the sharing and caring increased, so did the feelings of love. The three girls all seemed to play together well, and Jim adored Don. It seemed so right.

After dating for a year, followed by a six-month engagement, Holly and Don married. As their love grew, so did their desire to create a new life, symbolic of their union of love. Within the first year of marriage, Darren was born. Darren captivated Holly and Don as would any newborn. The next year flew by and, almost unnoticed, Jamie was starting to bloom into young womanhood as she entered her second year of junior high.

The first hint of problems came when Jamie didn't want to sit for Darren and Jim, while Holly and Dan went out to dinner. This was followed by Betty and Melissa getting into bitter fights and not wanting to be in the same room. Jim's teacher sent home two referral slips that said Jim had started two fights on the playground. A neighbor told Holly that she felt sure she had seen Jim smoking with some older kids in the alley behind her house.

Melissa started to talk back both to Holly and Don and refused to do her normal household chores. As the situation progressed, Holly occasionally inferred that Don was not really seeing what Jamie and Betty were up to. She had tried to say it in a reassuring manner without trying to be vindictive. But Don reacted. Countering with charges of the same lack of insight into her own children, Don became more defensive and protective of his own natural children. Holly then tried to shield Jim and Melissa from Don's sudden and unusual harshness.

Jamie, now thirteen, would storm out of the house for long periods of time and not tell anyone where she was going. Her friends now seemed to be from school only and not from the church's junior high youth group. The school called one day, asking that Don and Holly come to the principal's office. Jim had been caught stealing money from the milk machines in the cafeteria. Betty and Melissa were fighting so much that Holly finally moved Melissa into the basement where she slept on a couch. Wilting under the strain, Holly finally asked Don if they ought to separate so that things could be back where they were before marriage.

Ready-Made Problems

Territorialism

Holly and Don experienced a common malady in stepfamilies. Not only must step children progress through the normal losses of an intact family and the adjustments to a stepfamily but, as in the case of Don and Holly, they must accept a sudden and new set of siblings. This may seem to be cute and funny on the *Brady Bunch,* but in real life it can produce crisis.

Territorialism is common in children and, by the time they reach pre-adolescence, they have defined clear boundaries around the home. When single parents who have custody of their children marry, the forced brothers and sisters must mesh their territorial claims with their new siblings' equally-established territorial claims. This is confusing and irritating. Both sets of children are being asked to adjust to losses and gains in a very short period of time. Some of the losses are desirable, as are some of the gains. But, in reality, the children are asked to handle more losses than gains.

Accepting a New Environment
In a "yours, mine, and ours" family each set of children has not only lost their other parent but, of necessity, one set must also lose their home and room. They are asked to move into a strange house, most likely with less room and freedoms than they left. This is compounded by the fact that they must now share their remaining parent with a new stepparent and new stepchildren. It's almost like being last in line at the church potluck dinner. There are lots of nice things to look at, but there's not much left over when it's your turn.

Lowered Self-Concept
More involved problems may surface in the yours, mine, and ours family. Recent research has indicated that stepchildren may have lower self-concepts than children from intact families. Therefore, the potential for further lessening of fragile self-concepts is possible where two parents are striving to divide limited amounts of time between seemingly insatiable needs. Hence, some children may feel even more abandoned psychologically.

Coping Through Anger
What is devastating about this occurrence is that the manifestation of these feelings may be anger. But these are not the angry outbursts of a five or six-year-

old. In a situation in which a child feels seemingly ignored, that child may withdraw, act out in destructive ways, or become passive-aggressive. Some parents do not see these behaviors as signs of anger. Yet, each may be a primary indication that the child is becoming angry about feeling "second fiddle" and is coping in the only way known.

In the yours, mine, and ours family, withdrawal may take on many forms. The reason for the withdrawal is that a child feels abandoned over the loss of a natural parent through divorce, the subsequent additional loss of the second natural parent through a marriage, and the final loss of security and identity through the addition of new brothers and sisters. If a new baby is then added, the child may feel even further abandoned and unwanted as the joy of a new baby captivates the parents. Rather than trying to fight this on a daily basis and feel, what they perceive to be, daily rejection and/or lack of concern, the child may retreat in significant areas of his or her life that seem threatening.

Family involvement may be the first area to go. Missing dinner, avoiding family church functions, skipping out on family shopping trips, and shunning family recreational functions are typical. In each case, the child wants to avoid a situation in which he or she thinks that this apparent favoritism will occur. The wise stepfamily carefully constructs such events so that everyone gets a chance to ride in the front seat, sit in the special chair, or receive the new pair of shoes. Directly confrontational situations are some of the most devastating for the withdrawing stepchild. Finally, parents may expect even more of these problems as the children reach adolescence.

Acting out is to children what butter is to bread. They go together. Biblical parenting teaches that children's emotions are not the real problem, but rather the expression of them. Emotions are God-given and to suppress them in children is to deny the very essence of a child's humanity. Even the Lord Jesus Christ displayed emotions. He was angry, doubtful, reflective, and sad. Parents can use acting-out behaviors as a very positive teaching force with children, if they can recognize these as acting out.

Parents must remember that acting out is related symbolically to the problem of suppressed emotions. Thus, the child may not be truly aware of the deep inward feelings prompting the behavior. In the yours, mine, and ours family, a child may have the desire for the same amount of attention that he or she received before the new family came into being. Hence, the suppressed desires may be to get rid of the competition — stepparent and/or stepchildren. Therefore, the child may act out in situations that clearly pit parent against stepparent, or stepchild against stepparent.

Yet another tactic may be a reversal in school performance or general social behavior. The once good student in school may suddenly become a regular on the dean's list, the wrong dean's list. At the same time, the child may become involved with other children who are definitely not within acceptable guidelines. In the child's mind, the suppressed desire still may be for attention and security. Seeing that maintaining the applauded effort of previous years does not get the same amount of attention, because of increased sharing of parental time, a child may resort to opposite tactics to get crisis attention. The old adage, "The loudest squeak gets the most oil," is definitely accurate. The potential of this situation may become extreme if the stepbrothers or stepsisters have vastly different academic abilities or if they need extra attention and help. A "good" child may easily be taken for granted, especially if the parents feel like "that one" is all right and we don't have to worry about him or her.

Ready-Made Solutions

The task of raising a yours, mine, and ours family may seem impossible. It is indeed the most difficult to master and grow in depth and closeness. Yet, the Lord encourages the believer to let Him in on seemingly "impossible" situations. Surely Joseph felt some of the same frustrations when he discovered that Mary, his fiancee, was pregnant. Also, Paul reminds believers that how they think about a problem most definitely determines how they deal with the problem:

> *Do not be anxious about anything, but in everything, by prayer and petition, with thanksgiving, present your requests to God. And the peace of God, which transcends all understanding, will guard your hearts and your minds in Christ Jesus.*

> *Finally, brothers, whatever is true, whatever is noble, whatever is right, whatever is pure, whatever is lovely, whatever is admirable — if anything is excellent or praiseworthy — think about such things. Whatever you have learned or received or heard from me, or seen in me —put it into practice.*

And the God of peace will be with you.

I rejoice greatly in the Lord that at last you have renewed your concern for me. Indeed, you have been concerned, but you had no opportunity to show it. I am not saying this because I am in need, for I have learned to be content whatever the circumstances. I know what it is to be in need, and I know what it is to have plenty. I have learned the secret of being content in any and every situation, whether well fed or hungry, whether living in plenty or in want. I can do everything through him who gives me strength.

Yet it was good of you to share in my troubles. Moreover, as you Philippians know, in the early days of your acquaintance with the gospel, when I set out from Macedonia, not one church shared with me in the matter of giving and receiving, except you only; for even when I was in Thessalonica, you sent me aid again and again when I was in need. Not that I am looking for a gift, but I am looking for what may be credited to your account. I have received full payment and even more; I am amply supplied, now that I have received from Epaphroditus the gifts you sent. They are a fragrant offering, an acceptable sacrifice, pleasing to God. And my God will meet all your needs according to his glorious riches in Christ Jesus.

Philippians 4: 6-19

Stop Passive-Aggressive Behavior

Passive-aggressive behavior is a silent killer in stepfamilies. The angry child who handles emotions in passive-aggressive ways is potentially the most volatile. Parents will feel anger toward this child, but may not be able to pinpoint clearly the reasons. By definition, the passive-aggressive child works out his or her anger (aggression) in passive ways. Some of the more common ways are: being continually late with a seemingly good excuse, pouting for long periods of time without saying why, giving only half-hearted efforts to routine jobs, volunteering to do special jobs or chores but not completing them, procrastinating, and becoming abnormally aggressive when left in charge of brothers and sisters. Psychologically, this behavior stems from the absence of one or more natural parents and/or the presence of an overly-protective or overly-punitive natural or stepparent.

Similar to the withdrawing child, the passive-aggressive child may not feel able to compete with other siblings and may perceive this as unfair treatment. Typically, the child will then not talk about the angry feelings but look for subtle ways to show everyone how angry he or she really is. Some of the more prevalent patterns often involve authority. Particularly in the step-family, this involves new authority. Thus the stepparent often may be the object of the anger. The stepmother/stepdaughter relationship is commonly the most prevalent authority conflict in the stepfamily, with the stepson/stepfather being next.

Stepfamily development offers some explanation as to why passive-aggressive manifestations of anger may be the most common. At a time when the stepfamily is striving for cohesiveness and functioning as a unit, children of the stepfamily may feel grief and anger over the loss of their original family. As children move into adolescence, their needs for additional independence prompts parents to provide more freedom to facilitate their positive growth. In a stepfamily, parents are often tempted to place tight controls on everyone in order to get the new family "off and running." In their haste to get back to "normalcy" and "feel like a family" again, stepparents may lose vital sensitivity to the individual needs of children. The result is often trying to force everyone to feel like family. Then the battleground becomes clearly defined. The silent war is on.

In order to halt the silent hostilities, natural and stepparents must be willing to let children voice their feelings appropriately without reprisal. This, of course, does not mean that a child may say anything he or she wants and in whatever manner. The parents may define acceptable manners and inform the child that, as long as he or she stays within those boundaries, the discussion will continue. Next, parents must be willing to deal with the child's anger, regardless of what it is about. Hence, each parent must have resolved their own emotional issues long before attempting a second marriage. If not, emotional ghosts from the past will return.

With this commitment, the parents then may deal directly with the children's emotions. Critical to this plan is that the parent who is receiving the angry emotion is the one who must confront the child. Disaster is imminent when, for example, the natural mother says, "Now Bill, your stepfather knows that you are angry with him and he wants you to tell him all about it." Any enterprising child will interpret that comment something similar to this: "She finally got onto his case about being such a jerk. He really doesn't want me to tell him this, or he would ask me himself. So if I keep up the heat, maybe she will get rid of him and I will be number one again." But the child's actual verbal response will be, "There's nothing wrong, Mom. Everything is cool." Then comes the next round! Thus, not only must the emotion be dealt with directly, but the actual family members involved must deal directly with one another.

Be an Assertive Parent
An additional tactic is for the parent involved to say or verbalize his or her own feelings. If the stepparent, for example, is feeling as if the child is resisting him or her, he or she should say it. "Bill, I really feel like you are very angry right now, but that you don't want to talk about it. I feel hurt and cheated, because you are not willing to at least try." In this way the child sees the opposition as a caring and emotional person and not a silent adversary.

Use Contracting
Finally, offering to let the child develop solutions for some of the problems may open the communications gate. If chores are a problem, let the child propose a fair chore schedule with appropriate rewards for compliance and disciplines for not complying. This type of contracting helps the child to develop some self-concept through feelings of self-

accomplishment. If this is done with the adversary parent, the child may feel as if he or she at least is dealing with a fair person and the potential for developing into friends is growing. In any matter that arises in which passive-aggressive behavior has become the outgrowth of poor self-concept and subsequent anger, this method offers a sound solution.

Since this method can be such a useful tool, further explanation is necessary. Just as labor unions and management negotiate contracts in which both sides receive privileges and assume responsibilities, the stepfamily creates a similiar agreement. It is even advisable to write out the contract and have everyone sign it. Even if some of the children can make only a mark, let them sign it.

The actual contract is divided into two columns. In the left column is the heading "Rules and chores for parents and children," and in the right column is the heading "Responsibilities" or "Consequences." Then, father, whether natural or step, acts as moderator and asks each family member to write down specific chores and rules that he or she should do or follow. Once the rules and chores are established, father asks each family member to determine the consequence or punishments that he or she should receive for breaking the rules or not doing the chores. Often, the children will be harder on themselves than the parents would have been.

After the contracting is completed, father and mother may go over the contract to determine if it is fair and reasonable. If the contract is too strict or too lenient, then they must make the necessary changes, with father informing the family of the changes. If the contract is satisfactory, then it is implemented. Especially true for the stepfamily is the need for the parents to be in the contract as well. This will certainly promote parental respect and a cooperative spirit in the yours, mine and ours family.

The contracting process is also a rich opportunity for the father to assume leadership in the yours, mine and ours family. He may gain this leadership by consistently enforcing the contract that the family has negotiated. There is not need for him to nag and yell, but just to enforce the contract. If someone breaks a rule, enforce the contract.

Making the contract good for two-month periods of time, with weekly family conferences, helps to keep the contracting moving smoothly. At the end of the two-month period, if the family has done well, then father may allow more freedom in negotiating the next one. If it has not gone well, then father may make the new contract a little stricter. But if father is fair and consistent, the possibility that the contract will work is certainly enhanced.

Does mother have a part in the contracting? Yes, her support of father is essential. It will not work unless she is in total agreement. Her input and suggestions are mandatory. If she disagrees with father, it would be best to discuss those differences privately. Seeing mother and father acting as a team with father assuming the role of leader is critical for the success of the contracting and for the success of the yours, mine, and ours family, as well.

Wise Preparation

Be Patient Before Marriage

The yours, mine, and ours family is the most difficult to function. Therefore, single parents must realize that starting such a family may take longer than others. The most critical time is the period before the marriage. Following some of the previous suggestions of telling children about a new mate, the parents then must move into the marriage very carefully.

Plan Joint Family Activities

Before the actual engagement, it would be helpful to plan some activities involving both sets of children. In this way, two things may be learned. First, the parents may observe some potential clashes among the children. Second, they can observe each other and how each relates to the children. With this information, they can discuss their observations in private and offer suggestions for improving weak relationships or tactics. Often, single parents are in such a rush to marry that they forego this important fact-finding time.

Start Family Nights

Establishing a regular family night together before marriage helps the children in each family to assimilate the other children into each other's lifestyles. During one of these activities, the parents may then share their intentions to marry. But to leave it there is not satisfactory. Following the announcement, the parents need to let the children know that there is much to plan and decide. Because of this, the parents should tell the children that every week they all are going to get together with lots of pizza and soda (brain food for kids) and talk about some of the things that need to be done in order for everyone to live together after the marriage.

In order to help this family group to start, the parents may ask each child to write out on a piece of paper one problem that they are concerned about and want discussed. Parents may take turns reading these notes and then asking if whoever wrote each one would like to explain the problem. If the child does, then he or she gets the floor for as long as it takes to explain. From this, the parent then leads everyone in a discussion with the intention of resolving the problem. Issues such as who sleeps where and with whom, who gets the bathroom first, and who has to wear hand-me-down clothes may come up. Deeper issues, such as privacy, especially when a natural parent visits, also must be decided.

As these "nuts and bolts" issues are resolved, the parents may then move onto other areas. For example, they may encourage the children to share in the group some of the problems they have at school or socially. In doing this, each child has the opportunity to begin the new family with an awareness of the special needs of the other members. Then, he or she may not feel as left out when a parent gives extra time to a stepchild's particular need. Children may also be included in deciding on where to live and how the living quarters will be divided.

Even further potential problems may be addressed. Responsibilities and privileges, chores, and jobs are good topics. Since two different households and lifestyles are being combined, many compromises will need to be made. Again, this is a good time for the stepparents to take an active leadership role and earn the respect of the stepchildren. Being open and vulnerable about his or her own feelings about the new family will certainly encourage respect and acceptance. Holidays and vacations are children's as well as parents'. Therefore, they must be included on the agenda, as well as special activities.

Include Children in the Wedding Plans

Finally, a valuable way to encourage all of the children that both parents really want the family to work together and accept one another is to let the children help plan the actual wedding. That doesn't mean that they make the decisions entirely, but do include them in the planning.

Continue Family Conferences

To stop this family communication after the wedding would be unfortunate. Fantasy becomes reality when actual family living begins. In true American fashion, the best plans suffer from the trials of reality. Therefore, the family meetings are a must. There is, however, one exception. Any person has the right to call a family meeting, which means an emotional teen may call a meeting and then forget why by the time the meeting comes about. But in giving this type of positive reinforcement initially, the number of meetings will most likely decrease over time.

Yours, mine, and ours families may not be the *Brady Bunch*. Not everything will work out in thirty minutes. But planning and prayer with the Lord's guidance will help the yours, mine, and ours family not get canceled after three or four episodes. "Growing in step" can happen even in this special hybrid family. It just takes a patient growing season.

CHAPTER SEVEN

The Third Parent In The Family

Sid and Ellen, and Eve

"I'll answer it," Sid said, and picked up the phone in the living room. When he realized it was Eve, his former wife, he groaned. He and Eve shared joint custody of their children. Now that Sid had married Ellen, his already difficult communications with Eve had worsened. Since the wedding, Eve sometimes called twice a day to accuse him of not loving the children and of foregoing his fatherly responsibilities. She even alleged that he had used the children for emotional support only until he got another wife.

Sid and Ellen had noticed each other first at a church missions banquet. Sid started attending the church because of its single-parent class. He also went because he wanted to give his children a church-oriented upbringing, something they were not receiving when they stayed with their mother. After a courtship heavily involved in church activities, Sid and Ellen were married in a small church wedding. The children were given the option of attending the wedding.

Now that Sid was remarried, Eve seemed to have a new financial need for the children every week, in spite of the generous child support payments she was already receiving. One weekend, when the children were with Sid, his son Jason said, "Why have you stopped loving me?" When Sid assured him that he did love him, Jason retorted with, "No, you don't! You don't want to buy me the things I need any more. From now on I want to live only with Mom."

After this episode, Sid became increasingly tense at work and at home. Not wanting to burden Ellen with his problems with Eve, he remained quiet about them. He even started giving in more to Eve, just to get her off the phone. Although he didn't discuss Eve with her, Ellen sensed what was going on. She felt helpless, however, to do anything about it. She felt deeply resentful of Eve and became spiritually defeated over the matter. At times, sensing Sid's problems with Eve, Ellen would become critical of him, which only increased her frustration.

As these problems deepened, Sid's other children began to feel the insecurity of the conflict. They became more manipulative of Sid and of Eve to fulfill their need for attention. When Sid would discipline them, they would respond by saying they wanted to live only with their mother. Their remarks cut him deeply. Distraught and defeated, he withdrew not only from his children but also from Ellen.

Tom and Kara, and Hank

Kara and Hank had joint custody of their two girls, seven and nine. Hank had fought bitterly for joint custody in the divorce hearings, claiming he really loved the girls. This seemed strange to Kara, since Hank had given little attention to the girls during the seven years of their marriage. Seldom had he spent any time with them and he had avoided their shows of affection with excuses of having other things to do.

Although their marriage had been bitter and cold, Kara hoped that Hank would take the joint custody seriously. Maybe, she thought, now he wouldn't use the excuse of their poor marital relationship to avoid the girls. Now that she was out of his life, she hoped he would be a better father.

These expectations, however, proved unrealistic. Regularly, Hank would call at the last moment and back out of his time with the girls because he had to go to an "important business dinner." Three years in a row he promised to come to the girls' annual Sunday school program. He made it only once. Joint custody, on Hank's part, resulted in broken promises, shortened visits, and two little broken hearts. Nonetheless, Hank always prefaced each phone call to Kara with, "Kara, I really love the girls."

After three years, Kara met Tom and married him six months later. Tom was an excellent husband and was great with the girls. He provided spiritual and moral guidance to the whole family.

Tom disliked Hank adamantly. He believed that Hank cared very little for the girls and made promises to see them only when he felt deep guilt or loneliness. Kara, however, could not accept this analysis. Each time she talked to Hank she continued to be very accommodating, hoping that, this time, he would do something with the girls. At times, she even laid aside personal plans with Tom in order to get the girls ready to go somewhere with their dad. Each time, Hank would excuse himself at the last minute. Kara lamented that the only problem in her second marriage was how to deal with her first husband and his lack of relationship with the girls.

Third Parent Problems

With joint custody being prevalent in divorces today, difficulties like the ones given above are common with remarried couples. When a household breaks up, two new ones are established. With children living part of the time in both households or living in one and visiting the other, the potential for conflicts arises. Variations in lifestyle and discipline are to be expected. If these are not understood and handled well, they can quickly fuel new post-divorce battles, with the children becoming the casualties.

Revenge Seeking

The reason that the third parent in our new marriages is often so volatile is that the parental right of seeing the children is transformed into getting revenge on the former mate. All too often one parent champions a cause for "the sake of the children," when, in reality, it is an attempt to get even with an ex-mate. In turn, the children are forced to make decisions or allegiances that are unfair and harmful to them. Caught in the middle, they may deal with the tension between two feuding natural parents by withdrawing, acting out, or exhibiting passive-aggressive traits of procrastination, forgetfulness, and stubbornness.

Money Battles

The issue of joint financial responsibility arises quickly in this battle arena. Courts often award child support payments to the custodial parent, with various stipulations for other expenses such as schooling, medical care, and special needs. Often, this is not enough or it is poorly managed by the custodial parent. Instead of negotiating the issue in private with the parent who provides the financial support, the custodial parent may prime the children to ask the financial-support parent for more money for specific needs. If the support parent resists or refuses, the custodial parent may coach the children to believe that the other parent doesn't love them.

At first the children do not want to believe this, but later they may begin to accept it, particularly if the support parent continues to resist further demands for finances. Caught between the two feuding parents, the children feel anger, grief, and a deepening sense of loss.

Divorce Court Fall-Out

Unfortunately, the civil legal system is based on confrontation. As soon as the divorce proceedings begin, the battle is on and the two adversaries are pitted against each other. Settlements may be reached out of court but only after much emotional pain and legal fighting. This confronting spirit continues for years. Each encounter over the children sets the stage for the next battle. Reconciliation is a difficult task.

One reason why volatile confrontations continue after a divorce is that couples have the mistaken idea that, once the divorce decree is final, they will be rid of each other forever. Actually, divorced couples continue to have a relationship with each other as long as they live, primarily through their children. They may choose to stop being man and wife, but they cannot choose to stop being Mom and Dad.

Children in the Middle

Sometimes silence about the divorce can cause as much problem for the childen as open confrontation. If one parent openly discusses the divorce with a child while the other does not, the child may choose or feel compelled to side with the communicating parent. If neither parent discusses the inevitable questions that children have, they will still wonder and imagine about the issues surrounding the divorce, and will likely start blaming themselves for the break-up. Without parents knowing it, silence can cause children to put themselves in the middle, as the imagined cause of the break-up.

Children of divorce fluctuate between anger and guilt. Younger children, especially, feel the brunt of guilt. Too often, a child between six and twelve feels responsible for the parents' divorce. If arguments before the divorce included differences about discipline or if a child's behavior led to a parental fight, the children conclude that, had they not done what they did, the parents would not have fought and the divorce would not have come about. This guilt motivates many children either to dream about their parents getting back together or to actually look for ways to accomplish this. Some children resort to getting into trouble so that the parents will have to get together just to get them out of their trouble.

In order to avoid this problem, or at least to modify it, parents need to make a commitment not to finish pre-divorce fighting through post-divorce manipulation of their children. Ephesians 6:2 warns fathers not to provoke their children to wrath. Putting them in the middle of a battle that is not theirs will do just that. The same principle surely applies to mothers, as well. This makes it necessary for divorced parents to negotiate differences away from the presence of their children. If the divorce has been bitter and confronting, parents need first to forgive one another and then to ask God to help them deal with the bitter, confronting spirit that too often is an ugly legacy of the divorce.

Communicating with the Third Parent

Address Issues, not the Person
For a custodial mate who must speak to a support parent about financial, disciplinary, or privilege matters, the real issue is the children's welfare. The conversation must not be a psychological ploy to get something out of the other that could not be obtained before the divorce. No matter what, it is always right to do right. This becomes the cutting edge for divorced parents as they slice through a difficult part of their new lives.

Watch How and What You Say
Words and inflections often speak louder than the true intentions of the speaker. Certain words and phrases become staging statements for a confrontation and close the door to genuine discussion. Remember that "A gentle answer turns away wrath, but a harsh word stirs up anger" (Prov. 15:1). Before each discussion with the other parent, a divorced parent may need to pray for the words that will convey the real need.

Some harsh words that are used often to preface

child-centered communication are "You've got to," "Why haven't you?" and "If you don't." Instead of opening the door for discussion, such words cause a divorced parent to go on the defensive, feeling that they are about to be maneuvered and that the children are not the real reason.

Soft or diffusing words need not be "door mat" words, however. Those help no one. Diffusing words are ones clearly chosen to take the edge off potentially hostile conversation. One way to find out which words will communicate best to the ex-mate is to ask a simple question, such as, "When the children have a special need or there is a special problem, how would you like me to ask you about it?" There's no threat or subtle emotion, just a simple question about how the other parent would like to discuss these situations.

Stop Old Communication Patterns

Repeating past patterns of communication in post-divorce conversations is often a problem. These patterns lead to the same results they did in the marriage, none of which are positive. Divorced parents can give their children a present of love by avoiding destructive patterns of communication with the other natural parent. Regardless of feelings, divorced parents should develop a civil way of discussing child concerns, without putting the children in the middle of the parents' own past, and often unresolved, problems.

Commit to Financial Fairness

As previously described, the third parent in the new family often complicates matters. The two most difficult issues to master with the other parent are finances and discipline. Finances are critical, because our motivations in this area are affected by man's basic nature of self-centeredness. Jesus said, "For where your treasure is, there your heart will be also!" (Luke 12:34). A parent may say loud and emphatically that his or her only concern is the children, then balk at making financial sacrifices when those children have definite needs. Similarly, a custodial parent may use the supposed need for more money as a guise for greed, mismanagement, or revenge.

What then do divorced parents do about financial problems? Assuming that each is willing to work in conjunction with the other, a solid principle can provide children the same things and treatment that would be available if the family were intact. Just because the family is broken is no reason to increase spending on the children. The children may read this as a response to guilt, which will bring severe consequences in the future. In other words, spend as if the family were still intact.

If the true financial situation is difficult to sort out and the support parent fears the custodial parent is misusing the money or spending it unwisely, the support parent should try to send money directly to the source that will meet the need. For example, send tuition to the school, pay medical bills directly to the doctor, make payment arrangements ahead of time with clothing stores.

To stop being fair because the other parent isn't fair only hurts the innocent victims, the children. As Paul told Timothy, "But if anyone does not provide for his own, and especially for those of his household, he has denied the faith, and is worse than an unbeliever"

(1 Tim. 5:8, NASB.). Remember, it is always right to do right.

Commit Finances to God

When the financial-support parent is the belligerent party, then the situation, obviously, is more traumatic. How do you get someone to support who doesn't want to support? Usually divorce settlements state the amount and timing of child support payments. However, enforcement of the payments can be difficult. If the support parent leaves the state, there are few recourses to getting the money. Only recently has any effort been made between states to force a negligent support parent, who has moved to another state, to pay what the court of the first state has ordered. It's hard enough to get the state involved in unpaid child support cases when the support has been ordered by its own courts.

If support stops, the custodial parent needs, first, to ask God to intervene. After taking this step, the custodial parent should then keep the support parent informed, not only of the children's needs but of what is happening in their lives, as well. To call or write only when asking for money may infuriate the support parent. (In some cases, returning to court may prove beneficial, but this is a legal question that must be considered by a lawyer.)

In any case, the custodial parent must adopt an attitude of not expecting money from the non-paying parent. To continually expect something that does not come only produces more and more anger in the custodial parent. At this point, giving the situation to God and expecting and seeing Him work is the only peace-giving alternative.

Do not be anxious about anything, but in everything, by prayer and petition, with thanksgiving, present your requests to God. And the peace of God, which transcends all understanding, will guard your hearts and your minds in Christ Jesus.

Philippians 4:6, 7

Establish Mutual Discipline

Another difficult area to work out with the other natural parent is that of discipline. One parent may be lenient while the other is strict. In some cases, one parent, in a vengeful or vindictive manner, may be lenient or strict in direct opposition to the other parent's practice. Curfew, entertainment, friends, and freedoms are the "big four" involved in discipline differences.

Obviously, the healthiest way to deal with these is to approach the ex-mate and state that these different practices are hurting the children, so it is necessary to work out mutual practices for their sake. Suggest that each of you list your discipline practices and the reasons for them, and then compare notes. Then agree on common disciplines and consequences. If there is disagreement still, suggest enlisting a pastor, a counselor, or other neutral person to direct the compromises. In the end, the children are the ones who will benefit.

Again, while ideal, making such compromises is not the norm. Few divorced parents are willing to do something after the divorce that they could not do during the marriage. When compromise doesn't happen, direct tactics are the only solution. Painful as it may be, one parent may need to confront the other about harmful tactics.

If confrontation is needed, Ephesians 4:15 admonishes, "But speaking the truth in love, we are to grow up in all aspects into Him, who is the head, even Christ." This is important to remember during a confrontation. Name calling, unfair judgments, exaggerated examples, and character assassinations are not in keeping with the spirit of this verse. If a direct tactic is to have any effect, confronting the other natural parent with an attitude of calm, controlled truth will certainly give it the best chance of success.

But what about the "in love" part of "speaking the truth in love?" To love someone who is now an "ex" may be difficult. Two attitudes of love, however, must be present to keep a confrontation on course. First, accepting the other person as one whom God loves, in spite of what they have done (which is the only way God can love any of us), is one love attitude. Second, realize that, for the sake of the children, confrontation must be done in this biblical manner. What good is accomplished when a confrontation ends in a verbal battle between the two combatants? By consciously choosing to practice these two attitudes of love, a confronting parent can "speak the truth in love."

When there is no communication between divorced parents, confusion and disruption surely follow. If there is no communication, children may try to manipulate one parent with the statement that the other lets them do something, or that the other doesn't believe in a particular discipline, which may or may not be true. When this problem occurs, the parent needs to sit down with the children and calmly say that he or she has different ways of doing things, and then explain the reasons why.

At this point, incorporating biblical principles into matters of discipline are critical. In doing this, the child has the opportunity to see through parental disagreement. Of course, the child may not always take this opportunity. Emotional demands run high at this point and children may or may not grasp the true meaning of differences in disciplinary practice. Whether or not the child grasps this point, be sure to share the reasons, anyway.

It is important, also, that a parent doesn't put the other parent down through criticism or other judgments. This does nothing more than force the child to concentrate on the emotional differences between the two feuding parents and not on the merits of the decisions. They will see only the parent's anger and not the reasoning behind the practice.

In some cases, the conflict with the third parent in the family may become extreme. This could result in children being caught in the middle and hopelessly confused. A typical emotional response is for the children to react negatively to both feuding parents. Pitting parent against parent is common. Ten-year-old Carl answered his father's discipline with, "I want to live with Mom." If this situation continued to deteriorate, a solution is to call the child's bluff and to let the child make a choice. Vital to this step, of course, is to inform him or her of the consequences of that choice. (Using family contracting as described in Chapter Six may be helpful.) Yes, this would be a tough step. But sometimes, love must be tough!

The primary thing to remember, when attempting

to work out differences between the third parental practices, is not to allow anger toward the third parent in the family to hinder good parenting. When that happens, then "growing in step" is stunted.

CHAPTER EIGHT

Outside Looking In

Case Study: Pushed to the Outside

Jack was living in a small rented apartment, about ten minutes away from the house that he and Mandy had shared for twelve years. After their divorce, he had decided to stay in the area because of his job and to maintain contact with the children. Samantha was now fifteen and Jess was twelve. Many nights Jack would be in his apartment, consumed with loneliness for his two precious children. The pain was intensified when Mandy married Harold a year after the divorce. The kids really liked Harold and soon seemd to grow away from Jack. Jack felt his life was passing away from him even though his responsibilities at work and at church were going well. He couldn't understand why the children didn't want to spend time with him.

Case Study: Odd Parent Out

Maurice had remained single for two years following his divorce from Clair. He had maintained contact with their three children, although he would have liked to have seen them more often. But when Ginny came into his life, time was so precious. The pain of his previous marriage seemed to melt away in the open tenderness of Ginny's spirit. He really didn't realize that he was spending less and less time with his children. When he did see them, he always had Ginny with him and the conversation seemed to be about Ginny and their relationship.

So when the call came that Sunday afternoon, it really took Maurice by surprise. His former wife called to tell Maurice that the children had requested that they not have to go see Dad. As a matter of fact, they really didn't want to have to return to his house ever again. Their new dad was fine and they didn't want to have to interrupt their busy social lives to go see "him."

Closing the Emotional Door

Not all non-custodial parents want to be rid of their families. Many still want to be involved with their children. But what do parents who are on the outside do when their children don't want to see or spend time with them? Court orders may state that the non-custodial parent has the right to see the children, yet court orders cannot legislate the heart and attitudes of children. When children take sides and leave a non-custodial parent on the emotional outside looking in, no one can force that to change. This is painful for the outside parent.

Opening the Closed Door

Being on the outside looking in is not a desired position. It often produces more pain and confusion than the divorce. But some definite actions may help to open the door once again.

Commit to Taking Time

As previously stated, children go through many emotional conflicts as a result of the divorce. After the dust has settled, one of the battle scars that may exist is that the children may not want to see one of the parents. Anger, guilt, resentment, and misunderstanding fuel the decision to exclude a parent. Some children may even feel rejected by the noncustodial parent because he or she truly didn't want them, in spite of whatever the court has said.

Reestablishing the broken relationship does take time. Impatience is anything but helpful; patience is mandatory. The children usually do not want the divorce. With a dedication to be patient, the outside parent should then become consistent.

Be a Consistent Outside Parent

Consistency for the outside parent is not necessarily centered around the "biggies." Remembering birthdays and important holidays is assumed and mandatory. Children have the tendency to expect those. Vital consistency in little things is the area in which the outside parent can earn needed respect. When an outside parent sends a "just because" card or takes the children out for an impromptu hamburger, it is death for the relationship if he or she doesn't repeat that same type of gesture again and again. One-time shots are interpreted as motivated by guilt and not love.

Struggles with consistency are common, that's nothing new. For the children, "one time shots" hurt more than nothing at all. Getting one's expectations and hopes up by waiting for another such act that never comes kills love and desire. Therefore, the outside parent should carefully consider each action and promise before offering it. One lick of an ice cream cone usually lets the person know what he is missing. When a child experiences a little, without the promise of getting more, the pain becomes unbearable and something to be avoided. Considering Paul's admonition to do all for the glory of God offers instruction for the outside parent who is struggling with motivation and consistency in dealing with children. "Whether, then, you eat or drink or whatever you do, do all to the glory of God" (1 Cor. 10:31, NASB).

Recent researchers have spoken of the parallels between a small child's concepts of God and of his own father. These same researchers indicate that the parallels are strikingly similar. If a natural father is cold, removed, and distant, the children of these fathers often express that they feel that God is impersonal and not concerned about daily details of life. Even God instructs parents, and especially fathers, to teach and to model His character and teachings. Proverbs 4:1-4 tells parents that they are teaching in God's behalf:

Listen, my sons, to a father's instruction; pay attention and gain understanding. I give you sound learning, so do not forsake my teaching. When I was a boy in my father's house, still tender, and an only child of my mother, he taught me and said, "Lay hold of my words with all your heart; keep my commands and you will live."

Is it then any wonder that children often see parents, especially their father, as very much like God? Could Paul have had this in mind when he wrote Ephesians 6:4 (NASB)? "And, fathers, do not provoke your children to anger, but bring them up in the discipline and instruction of the Lord." Notice that the contrast is between provoking anger in children and raising them in the nurture and admonition of the Lord. Could one of the consequences of not being consistent with children in the role of an outside parent be not only parental anger, but some unrecognized anger toward God? All too often this happens.

Become a Courteous Parent

Consistency's first cousin is courtesy. For the outside parent, courtesy must often be preceded by the giving of it. How can an outside parent be courteous? Even though a child may be a biological offspring, that does not give an outside parent the right to be disrespectful to a child. Consider a child's feelings. Make plans ahead of time, not at the last moment. Call and talk to the child on the phone, not through some third party. When the outside parent has the children, he or she must respect their privacy. To barge into their room without asking for permission, or at least announcing oneself, is disrespectful. Remember, we are talking about children who don't want to be with the outside parent. To pull rank and force a parental way may end in disaster.

When children feel that an outside parent is respecting them through sensitive courtesy, the possibility of that being returned is much higher. If plans change at the last minute and an outside parent cannot make it, then the same courtesy that would be shown to a friend, business partner, or wife is mandatory for the children. An apologizing card, note, or gift is common in the adult world as a way of saying. "I'm sorry." Why can't it be the same in the outside parent/child world? Courtesy still goes a long way.

Paul gave the same advice in Philippians 2:3 (NASB). "Do nothing from selfishness or empty conceit, but with humility of mind let each of you regard one another as more important than himself." There it is again. It's always right to do right. Consistency and courtesy are two important social concerns for the outside parent. But still more important issues remain.

Recognize Betrayal Feelings

If the outside parent is struggling to regain a relationship with his or her children, the hurdle of betrayal feelings may need to be jumped first. For example, Kyle and Ken had lived with their mother for over a year after the divorce before they even considered wanting to see their father. Adam, the father, had faithfully called the boys during that year and tried to re-establish the relationship. Somehow Adam felt that the boys were angry with him, not Julie, their mother, over the divorce. Adam then realized that they were blaming him for the marital breakup. When he realized this, Adam sought some professional advice which proved to be worth its weight in gold.

The counselor pointed out to Adam that the boys may feel as if they were betraying their mother if they saw him. He added that the boys had already lost one parent and didn't want to lose the second by betraying her. With this insight, Adam then approached the boys in a more subtle manner. The next time he called the boys, he just said that he was going to be on their side of town on Saturday and wanted to know if he could stop by for thirty minutes. Adam carefully mentioned that he didn't want to take them anywhere, but just stop to see them for a few minutes. Hesitantly, the boys agreed.

On Saturday, Adam called them in the morning and said that he would be over right after lunch, if that was all right with them. When he got to the house, the boys were waiting on the porch. Julie was inside. After asking conversational questions about their week, Adam told the boys that he knew that they had a special relationship with their mother and that he never wanted to do anything to come between them and their mother. He thanked them for their time and left. He followed the same procedure for the next few Saturdays. On each occasion, he would remind them of his promise. He then added that he didn't want ever to ask the boys about Mom's private activities, since that would be between himself and Julie.

One Saturday several months later, as Adam was leaving the front porch, Kyle asked Adam if he would have time to drive him to ball practice on Tuesday evening, since Mom was going to be busy. Gladly, Adam said yes. On Tuesday evening, Adam drove by to pick up Kyle and, to his surprise, found Ken wanting to go along for the ride. That started a renewed relationship with the boys. Adam was careful never to violate the original agreement, since betrayal would always be an issue.

Adam learned that children may not want to betray a custodial parent. In order not to do that, they will avoid the outside parent. Therefore, the outside parent must understand the manifestations of betrayal feelings and work in the direct opposite manner. Assuring children of trying not to pit them against the other parent is vital. Next, making a commitment not to talk about or question the children about the other parent is essential. To do so puts them in the position of feeling as if they are betraying a loved one. Wise outside parents look for the betrayal signs and ask

God to help them to avoid them.

Respond to Negativism

Not only is betrayal a common problem for the outside parent, but in some cases they may have to deal with extreme negativism. This is usually much more than just feelings of hesitancy or betrayal. It encompasses bitterness, vindictiveness, and hostility. It is very difficult even to start to rebuild a relationship when children may not want to open an emotional door. Nothing is more disheartening for the outside parent than not to be remembered or thought of on holidays and birthdays. Usually this stems from some extreme conditions before the divorce and/or a bitter, emotionally-dividing divorce.

To reconstruct a relationship with children who don't even want to talk is an area of concern where the Lord must truly operate in both the children and the parent. No easy solution exists other than consistency, courtesy, prayer, and love. This may be love that is not returned, but nevertheless, there must be love. Consistently praying for the children will at least give the outside parent a spiritual fulfillment, if he or she cannot have the emotional and physical fulfillment provided by a restored relationship. If the custodial parent is then willing, the outside parent may ask for his or her cooperation in trying to reestablish a relationship with the children. It is essential to ensure the custodial parent that the only intention is to get back with the children and nothing else. Without the custodial parent's help, the situation is much more grave.

Re-earn Emotional Rights

An all-encompassing attitude summarizes the outside parent's posture. In this concept really lies the basis for the outside parent to reestablish a relationship with the children. Having to earn the right is difficult to accept, since the outside parent has a biological and legal right to the children. But far more important is the emotional right. This can only be granted by the children and not by anyone else. A parent leaving the home is devastating for children to accept. In their immature minds they often devise all sorts of reasons, judgments, and ideas about that departure. When coupled with the fact that children often are emotionally excluded during the last gasp of a bad marriage, the potential for establishing some deep emotional resentments by the children is possible. Thus, the parent who leaves may become the "bad guy." The custodial parent is the one who is remaining and caring for the child. Consequently, getting back on the inside may be an issue of earning the right to be back in from the children's viewpoint.

Of course, an outside parent has the right to see and be with the children. But that may not be the feelings of the children. "You left me" is something that may be removed or lessened only by much effort. Commitment to that removal is the fuel to spark the renewed relationship. To put a time frame on the task is impossible. Every child is different. Even children within the same family will react differently. One child who opens up to the outside parent before the others may face the others' wrath and abuse for "copping out." Throughout all of the efforts, the outside parent is wise in restricting them to the children/outside parent relationship. To bring in any other players to the cast is confusing and detrimental. This includes the mother, present wives and/or girlfriends, and relatives.

Turn to God When Lonely

The outside parent often is a lonely parent. Lonely the parent may be, but alone he or she is not. The Lord specializes in lonely people. He has been doing so since Adam and Eve. That is a reason why Peter said, "Casting all your anxiety on Him, because He cares for you" (1 Pet. 5:7, NASB). And if the burden is being an outside parent, God has a way of healing the wound and bringing emotional peace to an emotional cold war. Sometimes the "growing in step" seems to be lonely, but patient cultivating of the children may produce an emotional "bumper crop."

CHAPTER NINE

The Shake-and-Bake Family

Case Study: Ready-made Frustration

Bill and Mary met at the local grocery store. They literally ran into one another. He was turning into the canned goods aisle just as she was coming out. The result was a classic grocery store fender bender. Cans were rolling down the aisle, milk was running like a tidal wave toward the meat counter, and the eggs were already scrambled. The whole scene was so funny that they had to look at one another and just laugh.

Mary complimented Bill for keeping his cool in such a devasting situation. Bill mumbled something about the Lord helping him win with his temper, to which Mary responded, "Are you a Christian?" Bill's eyes lit up brighter than the cranberry juice now staining his pants and shirt. He answered yes and the relationship started. Both Bill and Mary had accepted Christ as Savior within the past few years. Both had been divorced about the same amount of time. Both had children.

Within the year, Bill and Mary were making plans to marry. Their "chance" collision in the grocery store started ten months of frenzied activity, which culminated in a small wedding with only the children and a few close friends present. Following the wedding was a brief honeymoon. Then, because both of them had to be back at work and the kids were in school, Bill moved in with Mary and her three children. Mary's children were sixteen, fourteen, and twelve and were constantly on the go. When they were not out, several of their friends were always at the house. On top of this, Bill's son and daughter occasionally came to visit for a few days. Bill and Mary didn't mind that there was always a lot going on around the house.

Mary's children's needs seemed to grow during adolescence, so Mary started investing more and more of her time in their lives. There were instances when Bill felt the bond between Mary and her children was too strong. Yet, he didn't bring this up to Mary, since his work was increasing and he had to spend extra hours at the office. Even those beautiful times of lovemaking that had been present in the early part of their marriage were becoming less and less frequent. These factors all weighed heavily on Bill as he closed in on his fortieth birthday. One Saturday morning Bill sat in the little coffee shop down the street, while Mary dropped off the kids at their various Saturday morning routines. Bill began to wonder if Mary really wanted and needed him or if he was becoming only a partner in keeping the house and children afloat.

Shake-and-Bake Love

Unconditional Love

Bill and Mary were experiencing many of the problems of the shake-and-bake family—the instant family. Their second marriage was not heading toward a divorce, but it surely wasn't growing in depth and intensity. Marriage is composed of several types of love. Paul wrote in Ephesians 5 that "agape," or unconditional love, is the dominating love that husbands and wives should have for one another. It is the type of love that Jesus Christ has for everyone.

Friendship Love

But there is more to the type of marital love that grows, enriches, and thrives. Scripture gives two other types of love that are vital to the strength of a marriage. Phileo love is the brotherly love that Christ had for Lazarus, which is mentioned in Hebrews 13:1 (NASB) "Let love of the brethren continue." For a marriage to grow, the husband and wife are to be best friends. A thought-provoking insight into this is that, since there is no marriage in heaven, "At the resurrection people will neither marry nor be given in marriage: they will be like the angels in heaven" (Matt. 22:30), a husband and wife will spend more time being a brother and sister in Christ (eternity, to be exact) than they will be as husband and wife. Hence, husbands and wives are to be best friends who demonstrate the many friendly acts to one another that the Scriptures implore.

For example, Galatians 6:2 speaks of bearing one another's burdens. "Carry one another's burdens, and in this way you will fulfill the law of Christ." Philippians 2:3 encourages believers to esteem others better than themselves. "Do nothing out of selfish ambition or vain conceit, but in humility consider others better than yourselves." Additionally, Jesus often spoke of putting others first. Imagine then what this does to the marital relationship. Not only are husbands and wives to be spouses, but they are also to be best friends. In dealing with the specialized problems of the shake-and-bake family, this aspect of love is vital

Physical Love

Another aspect of marital love is described in Hebrews 13:4a. "Marriage should be honored by all, and let the marriage bed be undefiled; for fornicators and adulterers God will judge." This is physical love. From Adam and Eve to the present, God has placed a high sanctity on marital sex. The author of Hebrews describes it as undefiled. Part of the understanding of leaving and cleaving is that husband and wife become one flesh sexually. "For this cause a man shall leave his father and his mother, and shall cleave to his wife; and they shall become one flesh" (Gen. 2:24, NASB).

Shake-and-Bake Problems

Too Little Time

Now with these aspects of marital love in view, a better understanding of the problems that husbands and wives face in the shake-and-bake family is possible. As seen with Bill and Mary, they had very little time together. In fact, they had too little time together. Research has indicated that couples who wait at least two years before having children have a lower divorce rate than those who have children sooner. But in the shake-and-bake family, that isn't an option. This factor opens up other possible problems.

Too Little Bonding

The bond relationship betweeen natural parents can be very strong. For the stepparent this bond may be threatening. Because of limited time and a possible strong bond existing between natural parent and child, the stepparent may become "odd man out."

What may ensue is a gradual withdrawal from the stepfamily by the stepparent.

Too Many Responsibilities
Additionally, in a shake-and-bake family, many existing financial obligations are brought in. Both husband and wife may have heavy financial responsibilities. This may entail subsequent heavy work obligations to meet them. The stepparent may also have previous commitments to his or her own children which take money and time.

Too Many Complications
Just as first-time newlyweds are in the process of pulling up roots from their own parents and establishing adult identities, the shake-and-bake family is doing the same, although more subtly. Yet, this is not easy, no matter what the conditions. It is difficult for first-time newlyweds and, certainly, no easier just because it has been done before.

Newlyweds without children have the luxury of being together physically whenever they so desire. Sexual activity is very high because they do not have interruptions or complications. But for the shake-and-bake family, the husband and wife often find that their lovemaking is late, hurried, interrupted, and often unfulfilling. Privacy is at an all-time low for the husband and wife. Not wanting children to hear or not wanting to be interrupted, lovemaking is often foregone. Since sexual fulfillment is a vital ingredient in a marriage, the marriage may start off not "hitting on all eight cylinders."

Too Little Adjustment

A subtle happening in the shake-and-bake family is one that isn't really recognized. Any marriage needs time for adjustment, recommitment, and stabilizing. Yet the shake-and-bake family places many demands upon the husband and wife that render time to do this impossible. A short honeymoon or even a long engagement is not enough time for each mate to see how much they really love, need, and want the other person. In some cases, the only needs and wants that come through are the need to help financially, the desire to assist in discipline, or the wish for some adult conversation at the end of the day. All of these contribute to a slowly eroding relationship in God's ordained institution.

Making the Shake-and-Bake Family Healthy

As Adam certainly must have said when he awoke from the surgical sleep administered by God and saw the lovely Eve waiting for him, many divorced people likewise say, "Wow!" when they meet another special person after the devasting loss of the previous one. Too often, that "Wow!" becomes an "Ow!" Why must this happen? And how can a second emotional tragedy be avoided?

Use Biblical Principles of Marriage

Marriage is honorable and ordained of God (Gen. 2:24). Jesus himself went to a wedding as described in John 2. Is it then possible that the same attitudes and commitments that are expected in a first marriage are to be in a second marriage, as well? As mentioned in Chapter One, it is not the purpose of this book to distinguish the biblical grounds for divorce and/or marriage. This is to be decided by the individuals long before they ever consider a second marriage. But once that is decided, then the same principles for marriage apply.

Love the Mate

The first and most obvious, yet the most difficult, is that of loving the mate. If a husband and wife are to come first (second to God), in a first marriage, then they must in a second marriage too. In other words, in a shake-and-bake family, the new mate comes before the children. Scripture doesn't place children before a mate. If guilt, anger, or any other emotion is fueling the action of putting a mate second to the children, then it will surely backfire. This is not God's plan for marriage. God's plan is for mates to work together with the children. This is true also for stepchildren in the shake-and-bake family. If this isn't being done, then radical action is necessary. Some radical procedures to remedy this are described in Chapter 10 on the "Summit Meeting."

Yes, we know that children hurt emotionally over a divorce. Yes, they are the innocent victims of the divorce. Yes, they didn't ask for all of the upheaval. No amount of empathy can really understand the depth of their pain. But the negative aspect of divorce is that it does have consequences. Does that mean that God punishes divorced people for the rest of their lives? Of course not. First John 1:9 (NASB) works for divorces as well as for "little white lies." If we confess our sins, He is faithful and righteous to forgive us our sins, and to cleanse us from all unrighteousness." But, not doing the right thing after a wrong thing only brings another wrong thing. It is always right to do right. Prayerfully, shake-and-bake parents will choose to do the right thing, even if it seems tough to do at the time.

Thus, the right thing for the shake-and-bake family is for the husband and wife to establish a strong and growing relationship. This is mandatory. Recent research reported that college students who displayed the best adjustment to adult life were those who identified their parents' relationship as the strongest in their family. The students who had the lowest adjustment to adult life where those who identified the strongest relationship as being a sibling relationship or a sibling/parent relationship. Isn't it amazing how Scripture rings true? For Scripture teaches that the husband-wife relationship is the most important.

Wives, submit to your husbands as to the Lord. For the husband is the head of the wife as Christ is the head of the church, his body, of which he is the Savior. Now as the church submits to Chirst, so also wives should submit to their husbands in everything. Husbands, love your wives, just as Christ loved the church and gave himself up for her.
Ephesians 5:22-25

Husband/Wife Relationship
This may be so important that it sets the tone for how well husbands and wives handle parenting.

Instead of reading the above verses, Ephesians 5:22-25, as a separate section, start with Chapter 4 and read through Chapter 6 without stopping. In order of priority, it is evident that God places the orders as God,

110

mate, children, work. Remember, mates will be together with each other much longer than they will be together with the children. Therefore, creating a strong husband/wife relationship is the best thing that can be done to undo the effects of a divorce.

Prepare the Children
Some practical things may be done before a second marriage. One is to establish a clear precedent to the children that the natural parent and stepparent will be spending time together alone. Children can then be reassured that their position will not be threatened, but that it is important for "Mom and Dad" to spend time alone. When children see that the new relationship is a strong one, then they may respond.

Inventory the Marriage
From time to time, the husband and wife may want to do some inventorying. Hence, they will ask one another if the children are coming between their individual needs. Only this open and vulnerable type of communication can truly benefit the marriage and the children. If the communication is difficult, then including a paster of professional counselor is mandatory. To forego this communication is a shake-and-bake family is surely to guarantee future problems.

Encourage Mates
In an intact marriage, husbands and wives help one another to grow through the various life stages that inflict everyone. It is vital that mates assist one another in negotiating two life functions: changes in

responsibilities and stresses of work and the difficulties of growing older. These transitional or life changes often intensify in a stepfamily and become even more important and critical. Long weekends away from the children may be the best medicine. If the children have to be sent to the other natural parent's, then so be it. Time, time, and more time is a helpful stabilizer for shake-and-bake husbands and wives. To sacrifice mate time for children time is not a sacrifice, it is a bomb!

Many wonderful things can happen on weekends without children that can't happen with them. Prolonged and tender, loving, intimate times without complications are a possibility. These become so important because couples need time to rejuvenate and evaluate. Returning to the shake-and-bake family after a weekend away fills the couple with new hope and determination.

Consider and Keep Priorities
For the busy obligated parents, constant decisions are to be made between family and job. Often work is easier to handle than coming home to the problems of the shake-and-bake family. First Timothy 5:8 (NASB) guides mates to consider their families first in all areas, not just in monetary provisions. "But if any one does not provide for his own, and expecially for those of his household, he has denied the faith, and is worse than an unbeliever." Paul used the Greek word *proneo* for "provide." It carries the concept of "thinking about beforehand, caring for," and "providing for." Notice all the ramifications of this one word.

First, "considering beforehand" would certainly

alleviate many family problems today if it were only done. Before words are said or time is committed, mates should consider one another and their children. Before additional job time is spent, they should consider the effect on their marriage and families. Often, a job decision is made with the long-term effects in mind, while a decision for the family is made with only short-term effects considered. In reality, the job decision is often more short-term, while the effects on the family are likely to be more long-term. Paul knew that not considering the family would have a long-term effect perhaps so severe that it would be like denying the faith or being an infidel.

Somewhere in the confusion and frenzied activity of the past twenty years, the concept of quantity of time with family and mates has disappeared under a blanket of material gain. Some maintain that quality time is an adequate substitute for quantity. Yet, the current increasing trend of divorce, depression, loneliness, and suicide in the midst of unparalleled material gain and leisure, surely indicates that something is amiss. This is even more evident in the shake-and-bake families where time is critical.

The country cannot return to the agrarian culture that is its roots, but we certainly can learn something from these roots about quality and quantity. During those long evenings after the day ended, agrarian families spent great periods of time with one another. No one rushed to his room to watch a favorite TV program. Churches did not draw the families out every night to another activity. Parents did not hurry off to a second job to be able to pay for the boat, the second car, or the pool. This agrarian type of time commitment is needed in today's shake-and-bake families.

As these families try to establish a new home under some very difficult and trying circumstances, they would survive and grow if the right priorities were maintained. Consider what effect the priority of family has over television, boats, cars, or new homes. Very few children, even stepchildren, would trade things for quality-and-quantity time with parents. Remember that Paul assigned priority to thinking ahead of time about the needs of the family, their emotional needs as well as their physical needs.

Good Instant Families

"Shake-and-bake" families may be a funny, even derogatory description to some people. But just as modern-day technology has removed the time factor in preparing fried chicken, modern family stresses have created instant families. Society is now heavily comprised of families who spring into existence overnight through remarriages. Some may say that something is lost because of it. This indeed may be true. It does not have to be, however, if parents of these families would remember the the same truths for a first-time marriage apply for a second. If these Shake-and-Bake parents would keep biblical priorities in perspective, and consider beforehand the consequences of their actions on members of the family, the "chicken" can turn out just as good.

CHAPTER TEN

The Summit Meeting

Case Study: Marrying into Cold War

Open confrontation is a characteristic of step-families, but productive confrontation often may not be the result. Such was the case of Charlie and his stepson, Scott. Charlie and Kristen married five years after Kristen's first marriage ended. Charlie had been single until he married Kristen. Her son Scott was twelve when they were married. Things went downhill with him from the beginning of the marriage. First, there were problems in school, then lying and passive resistance to Charlie's authority. Scott would often fail to do simple chores and explain it away with the excuse of "I forgot," "I was busy," or "I didn't have time." When Scott did do a chore, Charlie could count on having to do it over himself.

Charlie and Kristen tried every tactic in the book: rewards and privileges, then groundings, removals of privileges, and threats. All failed to bring about the desired results. When Charlie and Scott tried to do anything together the event would end in tragedy. Kristen tried her best to explain Charlie's feelings to Scott and Scott's to Charlie. However, she often found herself in the middle of a bitter feud where both of them were angry at her. Then, after five years of marriage, Kristen became pregnant and had Alicia

Charlie gravitated toward his little daughter and away from Scott. Gradually this distance became a gulf and all communication between the two ended. Kristen worked herself into a depression trying to get them together. Her spiritual life suffered and she withdrew from her active social life. Yes, she too loved Alicia. She had always wanted a daughter, but she also had another natural child to love. Charlie didn't and it was showing.

When Scott became involved with drugs, Charlie was almost uncontrollable. When he found out also that Scott was involved sexually with two underaged girls, Charlie gave up. He told Scott that he was a bum and would never amount to anything. For the first time in months, Scott answered, or better yet, fired back. Scott accused Charlie of never wanting him, saying "the only reason you were nice to me before the wedding was to get Mom." From there both fired charge and countercharge. When Scott stormed out of the house, Kristen broke down in hysterical crying and sobbed for hours. Charlie went out and sat on the porch, wondering why he had ever taken on such a problem.

Charlie, Kristen, and Scott had a "summit meeting" but it was really Armageddon. Even in intact families, wise parents know that as children grow older they have greater needs for control and determination of their own lives. This is often more evident in stepfamilies since a divorce forces the child to start the normal separation process much earlier and more traumatically. Normal separation, as mentioned earlier, takes from six to ten years. In stepfamilies the whole process is often completed in just a few years, in fact, in just a few short months.

Case Study: Forced Independence

Children of stepfamilies are forced to feel the need to be independent early. Such was the case of thirteen-year-old Terry who saw his family break up and end in about six months. Four months later, his father remarried and he was back in a family situation with a new mother and new stepsiblings. In his mind, everyone expected him to be "grown up" and independent about the whole matter, so he started to demand and act out those feelings.

Summit Meeting Benefits

Eliminates Fears

As these needs grow stronger, a helpful strategy is to hold family conferences or councils. If it is done on a consistent basis, the benefits may be many and lasting. A family council or "summit meeting" helps to ease the separation fears that often come from a family breakup. An easing of tensions comes from the fact that each child is now going to have equal say in problems. With this security base, children and parents can have an open environment to learn how to negotiate differences, rather than battle over them. This is a process that helps to heal wounds, as well as to give the children a model for conflict resolution that they may take into their own marriages and adult lives.

Stops Hidden Alliances

Second, family "summit meetings" show the children, or anyone, that wedges should not be driven between family members. Once hidden alliances develop in a stepfamily, it may be hard to know who is on whose side without such a "summit meeting." Specifically, children try to put wedges between their natural and stepparents. The reasons are many of the same that have already been mentioned and their results are just as devastating. "Summit meetings" establish the principle that Mom and Dad (regardless of which is the stepparent) are a unit and will act as a unit. Seeing a parental team rather than a tag team instills confidence and security for the children.

Helps Self-Concept

Third, "summit meetings" can be a significant factor in reestablishing children's self-concepts, which are often damaged through a divorce. Both Jimmy's performance in school and his overall countenance changed drastically after his mother divorced his father. Jimmy's dad often left for long periods of time and, when he was home, he was distant with Jimmy. Feeling left out in his mother's ensuing courtship with Hal, Jimmy became almost a twelve-year-old hermit. He seldom came out of his room at night, content to play video games and read comics. When the family began to hold "summit meetings," Jimmy started to reenter the family's life. Within a few short months, he began to improve in school. Within a year he was back on track. He began to be a part of the family knowing he indeed had a position of importance in his new family.

A historical side note may help to explain the importance of prestige in the family meeting. God made humans to be social beings. He even stated in

Genesis 2:18a that, "It is not good for the man to be alone." Consequently, the first society that everyone is involved in is the family. Psychologists have stated for years that the identity that is perceived in the family may be the one that is carried for years. What one perceives about oneself from the attitudes in the family are a great molder of self-concept and future self-acceptance. Consider the family origin of the United States. The nation was primarily an agrarian culture with large farm families. Each member of the family was vital because each contributed to the overall well-being of the family. Food, housing, income, and protection were everyone's job. Everyone was needed.

In contrast, the urban family has greater difficulty in accomplishing the same concept. Urban families do not have the built-in methods to help everyone feel a measure of self-worth. Some researchers have made a comparison that a farm child today is a five- to six-thousand dollar asset, while an urban child is a fifty- to sixty-thousand dollar liability! As the nation becomes more materialistic and urbanized, it takes greater creativity to ensure that children are feeling adequate worth within the family. The basis of this solution is to center the child's concept of worth around his worth to God, which is irrefutable.

Teaches Problem Solving

Fourth, "summit meetings" help children learn to deal with problems in productive ways. Instead of resorting to immature methods like passive-aggressive behavior, lying, and avoidance, the children have the forum in which to learn adult or spiritually mature problem-solving. If the children see this as a definite alternative to destructive problem-solving, they may indeed want to use it more and more. Remember, most children like to feel important and more mature than they really are. Capitalize on these feelings and "summit!"

Promotes Maturity

Fifth, by establishing an atmosphere of open honesty, "summit meetings" help the children to grow in maturity. They will know that they have a viable opportunity to work out the major difficulties of "growing in step." Since children can be flexible and adjustable (sometimes more so than adults) these open meetings help them to feel the security that they may need to get back on track toward maturity. If the meetings are held openly and honestly, the children will see the stepparent as a real person, and not so much a threat. When this happens, growth is inevitable.

Summit Meeting Rules

As with many things in life, timing is critical to the "summit meeting." If possible, "summits" would be ideal if they were started as soon as the engagement is announced. If the children realize from the start that they will also have position and a voice in the new family to be, some of the many difficulties that may follow can be eliminated. Assuming that "summits" do not get started before the marriage, the next best time is as soon as "the dust settles" following the marriage. With the many changes and the excitement of the marriage, children often feel excluded and threatened. As soon as it is feasible, start the "summit meetings."

Rule One: Pick a Time Convenient for Everyone

Specific timing is vital. One stepparent chose Saturday afternoon to start the meetings. When no one showed up except himself, he was furious and decided the whole idea was a farce, so went back to his old destructive ways. But what child wants to give up a Saturday to come to a family meeting? One stepparent tried to work a meeting in during halftime of a televised football game! Usually weekends are not the best time to hold such important meetings. A convenient week night is preferable. If that is not possible, then the weekend will have to do.

Rule Two: Be Consistent

Sometimes "summit meetings" are like diets. Many are started but few are finished. Making a commitment to conduct them on a weekly basis for at least six months establishes many precedents in the stepfamily. If everyone knows that they are important and give everyone an opportunity to resolve conflicts, "summit meetings" may become as important as Monday night football or the weekly shopping trip. After six months, everyone will know that the system works, so they will use it for conflicts. Then the meeting can be changed to an "as needed" basis. What has begun happening as a by-product is that family members are resolving problems privately without needing the security that the "summit meeting" provides.

Rule Three: Provide Something Fun to Eat

When churches want to attract crowds, they often use food. Jesus did. Family "summit meetings," therefore should be no different. Wise parents sweeten the attraction with sweets, pizza, or some other favorite food! People feel less hostile when their stomachs are full. This helps to remove some of the initial fear of it being a kangaroo court.

Rule Four: Inform Everyone

Make sure everyone knows the exact place and time for the meeting. Passive-aggressive children get lost and cannot find, or even remember, where the meeting is to be held. Make a poster, send out invitations, do whatever is necessary to make sure that everyone is there. With the logistics in place, the "summit meeting" is set.

Rule Five: Establish Ground Rules

Opening the meeting is not to be done with the intensity of the opening session of the United Nations. The "summit meeting" is not a peace-keeping team but a growth forum. It is important for both parents to share in explaining what is going to happen. Children need to see that it is the idea of both parents and not just the whim of one.

Before allowing the children to help join in setting ground rules, parents need to explain that the purpose of the meeting is to help everyone feel like a part of the family and to provide a place to discuss any and all problems. Openness is so important at this point. The children must be encouraged to share any problems, within limits. Expecting this to have an immediate impact is naive, but over a period of time this attitude will help break down barriers.

Father Leads Summit

One final necessity is to set actual rules of conduct. During the meetings that follow, the father, whether natural or step, should moderate the meeting. If the father has difficulty doing the actual moderating, then he may want to seek professional help. In doing this, the children are learning to deal with male authority figures, which are often the cause of many future problems. This is a must whenever possible.

Father then asks the rest of the family for rules they would like to add. For example, the family may decide that name calling and yelling are not acceptable. Writing these rules down and making sure that everyone understands them will help to avoid future violations. When there is a violation, allow the family to decide the consequences of breaking the rules. (This procedure follows the family contracting example in Chapter Five.)

After the family has discussed and formed the rules, the father will want to add the following ones, if they have not been discussed. All complaints, grievances, or problems are to be written out on paper. If one member has trouble writing, that child will need help. Next, Father will say that he will read the papers and the person who wrote it has the floor for as long as needed to discuss the problem. After the person has finished speaking, then everyone will have a chance to discuss the problem. After all feelings are expressed, then Father will ask the family members to suggest recommendations for the problem. If there is not universal agreement on the recommendations after the family vote, then parents will make the decision.

Summit Hangups

Emotional Ammunition

It is important to ensure everyone that what is discussed in the meetings is not emotional ammunition to be used against someone later on. During a "summit meeting," sixteen-year-old Jason discussed his feelings of alienation from his stepfather. Three days later the stepfather became angry at Jason and accused him of not doing something because he did not want to be part of the family. This emotional ammunition exploded inside of Jason and separated the two further. Matters discussed in the "summit meeting" are not to be used in day-to-day matters, since that will encourage children and parents not to feel free in the meetings. Using "summit meeting" information maliciously tells everyone that no one can be trusted or believed. It shows everyone that the cold war is indeed a hot one.

Emotional Outbursts

If the meeting starts to heat up emotionally, Father is wise to call a time-out and have everyone take a short break. Putting a break in the action allows everyone to settle down and re-think positions. To stem the negative momentum is an important technique during these "summit meetings." This action also tells everyone involved that Father is indeed serious about the meeting working and he is in control. When children feel that matters are being discussed fairly, they often feel more at ease to share problems.

Communication Insecurities

Sometimes children are reluctant to write out problems because of fear or inability to clearly state the problems. Therefore, Father may want to give them some ideas in the form of questions to be answered. "What would you do to make the family life easier?" is a good start. Also, "What would you like to see changed that would help you feel more a part of the family?" Finally, asking the family to write out a problem that they are having with another family member is a sure-fire way to show everyone that the "summit" will work. At this point Father will need to ensure everyone that he himself is included in any complaints.

Ganging Up

Vital to the protection of everyone is fairness. To "gang up" on one family member every time says to that person, "This is a vigilante committee!" Spread out the problems equally. Similarly, Father and Mother are not to dominate the conversation. Most parents feel as if they have enough material to write another edition of *War and Peace*, but they too must be patient and follow the same guidelines. If the family votes by majority to spend the entire "summit" on one issue, then do it. But the vote is to be a majority vote. Father as moderator retains veto power. He, however, must use this power with discretion. Discussing with Mother privately the various aspects of "summit" issues before the talks begin ensures that this will happen.

Remember, Mom and Dad are a team with Dad assuming the role of leader. If, therefore, Father only uses the veto power in emergencies, the family will have the opportunity to see that he is in control but is fair. They also may realize that Father does indeed value their opinions and genuinely desires to steer the family in the best direction. In the final analysis, this procedure may turn "hot wars" into negotiated peace. If the family votes unanimously to spend the entire "summit" on one issue, then this is fine. But the vote is to be unanimous.

Summit Power Struggles

As with many how-to ideas, power struggles and traps will occur. All procedures and practices need modification. The "summit meeting" has just those types of power struggles and traps that must be identified and resolved.

Mexican Standoff

Bill and Terri attempted to conduct "summit meetings" with their family. Bill's two sons and Terri's son and daughter thought it would be a good idea. It was, until Bill and Terri turned the "summit meeting" into World War III and disagreed on almost everything. They were so convinced that the "summit meeting" would work that they both concluded the other person's stubborness was stopping the process.

Whenever mates cannot agree, they must get a

neutral party to arbitrate. Asking a pastor or a Christian professional can often relieve the stand-offs, identify hidden emotions, and point out blocks to real communication. Pride can get in the way if one or both of the mates feel that they must be right or are solely responsible for making the "summit" work. This trap will not only destroy the "summit's" effectiveness, but doesn't help the marriage and family either.

Be My Lawyer

During a "summit meeting," twelve-year-old Sammy became the great stone face and responded only with primeval grunts. Frustrated by the boy's apparent lack of cooperation, stepmother Nan walked out of the living room. As if the switch had been turned on inside his brain, Sammy stated, "I'm glad that she left. Nothing ever gets discussed with her around."

Then Sammy began to babble about the many problems in the home. Twenty minutes later he finished, looked at his dad, and said, "Thanks for listening, Dad."

Dad, of course, was beside himself. "Why didn't you say these things when your mother was in here?" Dad asked.

"She isn't my mother!" Sammy exclaimed emphatically.

"I know that, Sammy, but she wants to be your mother," pleaded Dad.

"She never will be. I don't want her to be. Please, Dad, couldn't we just do this together and leave her out of it?" asked Sammy tearfully.

At this point, the "summit" isn't going to work. Sammy didn't want to participate with his stepmother because of the many reasons that children may fear or are threatened by a stepparent. Working on the differences is more important at this point than the "summit meeting." The natural parent and children may need to seek professional guidance or, at least, an objective third party, to lead in the resolution. In the meantime, if the child asks the natural parent to handle a problem with a stepparent, the natural parent should tell the child firmly, but lovingly, that the problem belongs to the child. Directing the child to attempt first to resolve the issue with the stepparent is a must. Offering to handle it only foregoes resolution and reinforces the widening division.

When a child speaks only in front of the natural parent and not with the stepparent around, that child may feel that he or she needs the parent to be a lawyer. This child does not trust the stepparent or feels that the natural parent favors the stepparent. He or she feels the natural parent will not be fair in a discussion if the stepparent is involved. Thus, the child will talk only to the natural parent when he can totally control or manipulate the situation. Directing the child to resolve the problem with the stepparent pushes the child into handling these conflicts. This affords the child the opportunity to see that the stepparent does not have to be feared or mistrusted. Important to this strategy is the stepparent's understanding of the issue and subsequent sensitivity to those special situations. It is not the time to be overbearing and dictatorial.

Parent Filibustering

During a "summit meeting," stepfather John talked on and on. His "sermons" shifted back and forth between disseminating wisdom and shouting fire-and-brimstone lectures. When he took the floor, the rest of the family knew they were in for the siege of the month. When one child dared to look longingly out of the window at the neighborhood sandlot game, he fell under the all-knowing eye of John. What followed is a classic example of intimidation by threat. Over the next few weeks, the family started to fear "summit meeting" night. As a matter of fact, two of the children (one was John's natural child) chose the punishment for missing "summit" (loss of television for five days) over the pain of sitting through another ninety-minute oratory. Frustrated, John sought professional help.

During counseling, in which John tried to dominate verbally, he hinted at some insecurities he was feeling. Soon he was admitting that he really didn't know how to handle confrontations with his family so would try to out-talk them. He feared that if he let down his guard for even a few minutes, the family would run over him. Not having the right answer was extremely threatening for him. He avoided that situation at all costs.

In some cases, parents hide their insecurities or fears by trying to out-talk their family. Unfortunately, everyone in the family realizes this except the person who is doing it. Admitting this insecurity is the first step in resolving the problem. No parent is expected to have the answers all of the time. Only the Lord has that ability. When the rest of the family sees that a parent is willing to admit some weaknesses or difficulties, that parent's position is enhanced, not weakened. Admitting problems can be a strength, not a weakness. This type of vulnerability in the summit meeting tells the rest of the family that admitting problems is going to be all right. When an open atmosphere dominates, the "summit meeting" works. When one person dominates the meeting, the rest want to be somewhere else and "summit meetings" become another source of pain and frustration.

Summit Communicating

Staging Statements

Turning away wrath is the real purpose of Proverbs 15:1. "A gentle answer turns away wrath, but a harsh word stirs up anger." Soft words are the catalyst for diffusing heated situations. In some cases, the words spoken just prior to the words that stir up the anger are more critical than the anger-stirring words themselves. These initial words like "you never" or "you always" become staging statements that can move conversations into full-blown verbal battles. Since a believer has the power of the Holy Spirit available to control conscious thoughts and actions, the responsibility for the heated discussion belongs to the person who uttered the staging statements.

Just as staging statements shuts the communication door, soft and diffusing answers open it. While Hank was admitting to his wife that he was wrong and sorry, she kept on rehashing the problem. Finally, in frustration over Hank's sudden and sincere change in attitude, she looked at him and said,

"You can't be sorry yet. I am not done being angry!"
The door opening had worked. The message was
received.

Discovering Staging Statements

Discovering what are staging statements is
rather easy if one wants to know. During "summit
meetings" each member is given the opportunity to
write down on paper the phrases the others in the
family use that are hard to handle. Besides expansive
statements, often these phrases are pat answers or
sarcastic remarks. Once everyone has had an opportunity to write down these phrases that are so difficult to take, father asks everyone to agree not to use
these phrases. It is easy to point out that they certainly do not work and only increase tension. Therefore, eliminating them from discussions is the only
logical course. The family may want to vote on a
system of fines for those who choose to violate the
ban. Every six months the money can be used for a
family party.

Once the negative or staging statements are
used, the person who wrote down the other person's
staging statements can offer the user a more productive and less threatening way of expressing feelings.
This assertive way of sharing emotions works
healthy changes in the family's communications
pattern and does indeed turn away anger.

Summit Growing

The "summit meeting" is just that. Everyone
enters with equal rights to share feelings and problems. Obviously, the meeting will not work the first

time. Probably the meeting will take some practice, spread over a period of time, to be successful. The family will perfect its usage. Most failures in family living center around a lack of consistency and persistence. Learning from failures is vital to the eventual success of the "summit meeting." Allowing the family to analyze the mistakes promotes even quicker perfecting of the "summit meeting." Mixing in a measure of honesty, seasoning with a pinch of vulnerability, and adding two cups of consistency cook up a really great "summit meeting." This recipe produces a truly emotionally, nutritious way to "grow in step."

CHAPTER ELEVEN

Happy/Painful Days

Case Study: Alone Again

Sitting in the living room of his two-bedroom condo, David wondered if life could be any lonelier. Christmas Day had always been such a happy time in his life, that is, until the divorce. Now, the first year after the divorce found David alone at Christmas and without the three children who meant everything to him. The court ordered alternating holidays for the children, and Mandy had the children this year. David's parents were several thousand miles away and no one else lived near enough to him to make a visit feasible. How could such a happy day be so painful, thought David, as he drank his third cup of coffee and stared out the window.

Case Study: Where Are You When I Want You?

Fifteen-year-old Allen was ecstatic as he ran to the locker room. He had just led his team to a convincing 33-7 win over a major football rival. Allen had scored two touchdowns and contributed to two others in leading his undefeated high school football team to its seventh straight win. The coach had told him before the game that several major college scouts were watching his career and were equally impressed with his 3.5 grade-point average. Allen was feeling on top of the world. After a jubilant and rowdy locker room celebration, Allen showered and left to meet his family. In the parking lot, buzzing with excitement about a possible state championship, Allen met his family, well, most of his family. His thirteen-year-old sister Becky was standing next to his mother, who was holding hands with Allen's stepfather. The joy of that night's great success seemed to disappear in a wave of disappointment. "I wish Dad were here. I want him to know that I did this for him," he thought. Unknown to Allen, his mother, too, longed for Allen's father to share in this triumph. But Allen's father had stopped any contact with the family, even child support.

Case Study: Part-time Joy, Full-time Pain

"I cannot believe how much they are growing. By the time I see them again, they will be huge. They're growing up and I am missing it. I don't know if I can take it," thought Carrie as she watched her two toddlers waddle down the sidewalk and get into her former husband's car.

Carrie shared custody of the children with Ian, her former husband, but the arrangement was such that the children would be apart from her for a month at a time. She had already missed her four-year-old's birthday, since he was at Ian's during that time. The two-year-old had started to talk during the last stay with Ian and she had missed that tender milestone. For bringing so much pleasure when she had them, the pain of not having them seemed to be more. This is how it is going to be the rest of their lives, thought Carrie. That thought led to the rebirth of all of the divorce anger and despair that Carrie thought she had resolved. With tears pouring down her face and a big knot in her stomach starting to tighten, Carrie literally ran back into her apartment, wishing that tomorrow would go away.

Court-Ordered Pain

No other problem of divorce has the potential to be so thoroughly devastating as that of shared custody of children. Parents may often be consumed by the guilt of inflicting such deep pain on their innocent children. Then, to see those precious people taken in and out of their lives on a regular and court-ordered basis is overwhelming. Several factors make this now necessary aspect of living so unlivable.

On-and-Off Joy

First, when the children leave to go to the other parent, the house is suddenly cold and lonely. If a parent remains single, there is no one else to fill the emotional void that is left. Thinking about what the children are doing in their other home may fill long, lonely stretches of time. Even if the parent is remarried, the feelings may still be present. A new partner may not be all the parent wants at such times.

Missed Memories

Second, shared custody forces parents to miss some special times with the children. In growing up, there is not an instant replay. The parent who misses out does not have an opportunity to have the child do it all over. Sharing custody means sharing the happy days. Those that are happy for one parent, however, may be painful for the other.

Competing Influence

Third, accepting that another person may have influence in the children's life is a sobering and sometimes depressing fact. If the other parent is remarried, then the children will have another influence. This is beyond the control of the parent who does not have the children. New values and new ideals are being taught. Ideals in one home may not be compatible with the ones taught in the other.

Recycled Loss

These three factors are by no means exhaustive, but they point to one main result of joint custody. Separation from the children and granting them subsequent independence is started much earlier than in an intact family. Typically, children move into independence in the adolescent years. Wise parents realize this and start the separation process. In a joint custody situation, the separation occurs every time the children leave to go to the other parent. No easy solution appears for the separated parent's feelings. Surrounding oneself with caring and loving Christian friends is certainly a positive coping step. Christians display one of their great powers when they shoulder the burden of a brother or sister in Christ. "Bear one another's burdens, and thus fulfill the law of Christ" (Gal. 6:2, NASB)

Love from Afar

Parents in a joint custody situation have a difficult decision. In effect, they become part-time parents. But they may remain fulltime "prayer parents." To interfere with their time with the other parent by calling and/or dropping by is to put the children in a middle position. Wise joint-custody parents call or visit the children at the other parent's home by invitation only. The invitation may come from the children or from the other parent but, in both cases, the other parent must give total approval. This leaves parents with the opportunity to remain a full-time "prayer parent." Bringing the children before the Lord on a regular basis may be the only direct activity during the non-custody period. Investing in the absent children's lives by praying keeps emotional and spiritual bonding, even when physical bonding isn't possible.

Living Happy/Painful Days

The list of happy/painful days is long. It includes holidays, birthdays, special events, school activities, church activities, special achievements, and many more. Whatever should be a happy day and isn't because the preferred parent is absent is a happy/painful day.

Case Study: Money Pain

Other situations create happy/painful days. Karen watched tearfully as her two young children opened the one Christmas present that she was able to afford. Since the divorce, her former husband had made only one child-support payment. Karen often did not know from where the next rent payment would come. At times, she did not have enough money to buy the children needed school clothes. Money problems haunted her every day.

Case Study: Embarrassing Pain

Harry brought his mother and stepfather to the church parents' night. As each of the children stood to introduce their parents, Harry felt a growing uneasiness. How would he do it? Would the other children laugh? He really did not feel like calling his stepfather "Dad." Why couldn't my real father be here, he sighed in anguish.

Case Study: Missed Family Pain

As Jill and Jane walked into the house filled with laughing strangers, they wondered what the rest of the day would be like. Annie, their stepmother, promised that her relatives would accept them as if they were family. But still, Jill and Jane did not feel like "family." They would rather have had their real relatives for Thanksgiving instead of these strangers. So, much to the disappointment of Annie, the girls sat in the corner of the room for the entire time.

Case Study: Frustration Pain

Sue called her former husband to ask if he would be able to share half of the expenses of sending the children to camp. The children really wanted to go. Ed, now remarried, answered abruptly that he did not want to reply right away, but asked for time to think about it. Sue knew that meant no answer at all, since he seemed to do that with most matters involving the children. When she forced him to answer, he became enraged and said that she certainly could have asked this sooner. He said that she was trying to use the children to hurt him and he would never give in to that. If she wanted them to go to camp, then she should pay for the whole thing. When Sue hung up and turned to the children, they knew already that they were going to miss out on another fun activity because Mom and Dad still could not talk to one another.

Causes of Happy/Painful Days

Financial Dependency
Each of these situations are loaded with emotion and subsequent pain. Even when a parent has custody of the children, the happiness of having the children is often interrupted by the pain produced from not being an intact family. When a mother is dependent upon child support and the support is irregular or non-existent, the pain is real. Explaining to the children that certain things are not possible because Dad did not send the money this month may be explosive.

Four Sets of Relatives
Further, happy/painful days may include coping with four sets of grandparents and relatives. If both parents remarry, this can be confusing and difficult. In some cases, two of the groups of step-relatives may not even want to be involved. Also, a child may feel no greater pain than that of wanting an absent parent present in times of personal pain or triumph. This one factor may be a major contributor to the feelings of abandonment that are prevalent in many adolescents. In the midst of great joy, children may experience great pain because a desired parent is not present.

Conflicting Values
Differing value systems between custodial homes often produce happy/painful days for both children and parents. Anticipating time with the other parent may last only until the first battle occurs, because of differences in rules and regulations between the two custodial homes. Greg bounced into his dad's home

after Mom dropped him off at the front door. Once inside he yelled, "Dad, I'm home." His voice seemed to say, "I love you, I am glad to be here, I missed you, let's do something," all at the same time. When Ginny, his stepmother, yelled from the kitchen "Be quiet, we don't yell in this house," Greg knew he was only half welcome. The next week would be a happy/painful time for him.

Fallen Heroes

Fallen heroes are another type of happy/painful days. Children may often develop an unrealistic idea about the outside or removed parent. This may be produced by feelings of rejection, denial of emotions, guilt about the divorce, insecurity, and/or anger. Whatever the emotional reason, the children may not want to see the outside parent in a realistic manner. Often, the children will see the truth that they are trying to avoid and will have to view that parent in a more realistic manner. This is painful. The unrealistic ideal of the outside parent may be the way that the children keep the memory of the natural family intact.

Not wanting to let this go, children may use emotional defenses to keep some aspect of it intact. This often results in an idealistic expectation or view of the outside parent. If the situation is compounded by the outside parent using the children in a manipulative manner, to invoke hurt or revenge against the custodial parent, the problem is intensified. At this point, some clear directives are necessary to help in coping with an idealistic view of an outside parent and a possible fallen-hero problem.

First, the custodial parent should not defend or

put down the outside parent. This is something that the children must resolve in their own minds. To force recognition of the outside parent's faults puts the custodial parent in the middle. The children may not want to believe the custodial parent or feel the need to take sides. If the custodial parent is in the middle, the children see only the custodial parent and not the outside parent. Realism is painful, but it is therapeutic. Allow the children the opportunity to see reality for themselves.

Second, the custodial parent intervenes only in cases of safety for the children. If the custodial parent fears a definite threat to the health and well-being of the children, then he or she must get in the middle. At this point, it is wise to tell the children the reason for the action. Avoid judgmental statements about the character and purposes of the outside parent, but clearly state the reasons for the intervention.

Third, give the children the opportunity to see the outside parent in a true light. Idealism is modified under the scrutiny of realistic situations. To defend the outside parent in hopes of sparing children the pain of seeing reality is self-defeating. Children may become angry at the custodial parent for covering up by "lying." Let the children discover these things in their own timing and in realistic ways.

Recurring Court Battles

One final and specialized happy/painful day is that of going back to court. Custody cases are never-ending, it seems. In some cases this is true both legally and emotionally. But going back to court to clarify or enforce a custodial decree happens. First, consult a

141

lawyer. With the changing custody laws in various states, it is necessary to consult a competent lawyer to ascertain the merit of any proposed return to court. With the cost being high, both in emotional and financial terms, returning to court must be a prayerful and thoughtful choice. Explaining the reasoning to the children, therefore, is equally important.

Children want to know why Mom and Dad are in court again. Reliving the pain of the divorce is common for children each time their parents turn to a legal solution of current problems. Answer the children's questions. A long, involved explanation is not needed, but do answer their questions. As they get older and can deal with more of the emotions of a court action, then explain them. In other words, let the children set the pace for how much is explained. But do explain.

Do not use the court action as an attempt to put down the outside parent in front of the children. This is dishonest and unfair and is using them to continue to seek revenge against a former mate. Remember, it is always right to do right and this is not right. Paul was clear on this point when he wrote, "Never pay back evil for evil to anyone. Respect what is right in the sight of all men" (Rom. 12:17, NASB). Even the vilest of outside parents is no justification for seeking revenge or not doing what is right. Maintaining this attitude produces growth in the custodial parent's spiritual life and is a landmark guidepost for the children who see it.

A final consideration in a return to court is for the stepparent to take an active role in an explanation to the children. If done in a Romans 12:17 attitude, children may see that the issue is really one of principle and is a "right cause." It may help them to see that it is not an attempt by their natural custodial parent to get even. If both natural and step custodial parents handle the court case in a spiritually and emotionally mature way, the children may see that the case is necessary and right.

Guidelines for Happy/Painful Days

As can be seen, there are many types of happy/painful days. Remembering that happy/painful days are those times when the joy of children is lessened because it must be shared with a former mate, some coping guidelines are needed.

First, honor the terms of a custody settlement. Even if painful, they must be honored. Marriage and divorce are a legal status and must be honored as such. Therefore, when a couple divorces, they automatically put themselves under the control of the civil law. Not to honor the civil law complicates the problem. Read Romans 13:1-2 to see that Paul mandated that believers obey the law.

Second, be sensitive to the child's needs on happy/painful days. As children grow older, let them decide where they want to live. If the outside parent is a dependable parent and the children want to live with him or her, let them go. Holding onto them for emotional reasons increases the happy/painful days and may lead them into painful/painful days. When a child expresses a desire to be with a certain parent for a special day or activity, work it out. Help the child to have as few happy/painful days as possible. Not allowing children to have this kind of flexibility (as long as it is not a manipulation) is to victimize them all over again.

Third, avoid competing with the outside parent.

Attempting to make up for happy/painful days by outdoing the outside parent is destructive to everyone. It forces the children to make choices they really don't want to make or are not equipped to make. This would include gifts, vacations, toys, activities, food, and birthdays. The list is endless. The right motivation is to do what is right, not what is more or better than what the outside parent did.

Fourth, use happy/painful days to teach children discernment and understanding. This is best done by modeling the mature way to resolve adverse situations. If parents can be stable during adverse times, then children have a model to follow in dealing with happy/painful days themselves. An example of this is that the children can be taught that two views can exist about the same situation. In happy/painful days, the problem is often one of preference rather than of principle. Showing the children that other preferences may be possible instills the sense of tolerance that is a vital aspect of Christianity. In contrast, when a custodial parent must create a happy/painful day because of a biblical principle, children may then see the importance of taking the necessary stand. However, to make every preference a principle makes for many happy/painful days.

Fifth, create new traditions in the family to help replace or substitute for happy/painful days. Not all of them may be replaced, but the medicine goes down better with a little sugar on it. So create new happy days in the new family.

Sixth, teach the children that their true identity is being God's child through faith in Christ. Yes, they may have a confusing family identity, but their "true" identity is in God's family. "But as many as received Him, to them He gave the right to become children of God, even to those who believe in His name" (John 1:12, NASB). This is the family identity that helps any happy/painful day. Christ died, was buried, and rose the third day so that anyone by faith in Him may have eternal life. "For God so loved the world, that He gave His only begotten Son, that whosoever believes in Him should not perish, but have eternal life" (John 3:16, NASB). This is the ultimate happy day and the basis for living now.

Happy/painful days are as varied and unique as families themselves. Each family is different and each stepfamily is even more so. Understanding how and allowing the new stepfamily to grow in its own unique manner is "growing in step." As common as happy/painful days are, a wise stepfamily realizes, accepts, and uses them to produce growth that in turn shades the stepfamily from the pain of those days.

CHAPTER TWELVE

The Bond That Isn't There

Case Study: The Wrong Mother

"You aren't my mother and you will never be my mother," screamed twelve-year-old Amy as she ran out of the family room. Helen was both crushed and furious, but could not decide which emotion would reign. For the last three years Helen had tried everything she knew to reach Amy. Before thay were married, Helen and Will had discussed that Amy might be difficult to reach, since she had been so close to Will's former wife, Jackie. Even though Amy was only seven when Will and Jackie divorced, she was still deeply bonded to her mother.

Helen long to sit on the bed with Amy and talk about friends, dresses, boys, or school. But Amy was vehement that Helen not come into her room. She even refused to let Helen in the room unless she was fully clothed. Helen cried time after time over the rejection she felt. At thirty-two, she could sill have children but feared bringing another child into the situation as it was. Time after time she asked the Lord to show her how to have that special bond.

Case Study: Ashes to Gold to Ashes

Joe had always been a quiet, passive type of man. His former wife said that he had been too passive. But his two children didn't seem to care. Often Joe and the two children would lie on the living room floor and have wrestling matches. They would jump on Joe and try to pin him down as they all laughed uproariously. Many evenings would end with Joe lying on his daughter's bed and reliving the events of the day. After solving those problems he would go into his son's room and discuss the pennant races or motorcycles. Life was happy until his wife said she was filing for divorce.

Joe went into a depression after the settlement was final. He got the children only on weekends and for two weeks during the summer. At times he felt as if his very soul had been ripped from him. The next two years were lonely, including those emotional oases when he had the children. Those hours seemed to fly by in a race. Friday came and it was suddenly Sunday evening. Weekends were filled with fun, togetherness, and tenderness. Each night they would pray as a family and share how the Lord had blessed them during the day, Joe even taught the children basic Christian doctrines from his old doctrine book from Bible college.

After his wife remarried, Joe realized that reconciliation was no longer a possibility. To accept that required him to make some major assessments in his life. He had to reconcile his anger, guilt, and loneliness. At times he even felt angry toward God, because He had not answered his prayer for reconciliation. When the spiritual dust settled, Joe saw that his life was still under God's control and it would go on without his wife. A few months later it did go on and with a woman named Patty.

Patty started attending the church's Thursday evening Bible study. When Joe and several friends went out for coffee after one of the studies, Joe invited Patty to come. She, too had been married before but had lost her husband through death. At thirty-two, she was a widow with three children. From the first time he heard the details of Patty's loss, he felt a deepening compassion for this woman and her family. As he came to know Patty, Joe discovered a spirituality and sensitivity that thrilled him. Soon Joe and Patty were regulars at the Bible study and the coffee time afterwards.

Their relationship moved from the warmth and support of the Bible study to other parts of their lives. And that included Patty's children. To say that their reception of Joe was cool was like saying the Arctic Ocean is cool. In the children's minds no man would ever replace their father. The children had his picture in their rooms and their most explicit memories were of their dad and the things that they did together. Joe felt as if he were walking in the shadow of Superman.

The boys looked at Joe with skepticism and the girl often left the room when Joe came in. Knowing that the children were struggling with day-to-day problems of the pre-adolescent years and not opening up to him was painful to Joe. He longed to encourage, help, and support. But each attempt was met with rejection. Torn by the failure he was experiencing, Joe asked Patty if she felt they should stop seeing each other because of the problems with the children. Patty was equally dismayed about the children. If they could only see Joe as I see him, things would be different, she often thought. The problem was beyond the understanding of both of them. So confused by the problem were they that Joe and Patty broke off their relationship.

Bonding Blocks

While people remarry and create stepfamilies, many never experience the bonding of the family unit that is necessary for a blended family. Common assumptions are that the bond will just happen and that stepfamily bonds are the same as those of the intact family. Both assumptions lead to frustration and emotional pain.

Difficult Adjustments

In order of severity, the bond which is most difficult to achieve is between stepmother and stepdaughter. Research shows that more conflicts occur between stepmother and stepchildren than other relationships in the stepfamily. This can be attributed to the dominance of mothers in the early parenting years of the children. Even if the natural mother is working, she is still the most dominant day-to-day influence for the children. The woman who replaces that mother must be superior in order to overcome this maternal bonding.

In some cases, the children may be angry at the natural mother for leaving the family but do not want to admit or deal with that emotion. Hence, the stepmother, untrusted to begin with, may often be the scapegoat as children transfer their anger to her. When the stepparent is new father, children may feel that their mother has betrayed their natural father. But they will not deal with these feelings so may reject the stepfather. To keep communication open is mandatory. Often the children will be belligerent and hostile in their communications, revealing their deep hurts. Leaving communications lines open while teaching them how to share their hostile feelings is a bonding setter.

Peer Pressure

Beyond the parental bond are other factors affecting fusing of the family unit. Peer pressure from friends can be a deterrent to stepfamily bonding. Even though divorce is common among the children's school contacts, it may not be common in their church. Hence, the children may receive some ridicule in their church environment, which may be transferred onto the stepparent. This may even cause some children to react by not accepting the spiritual guidance and teaching of a stepparent.

Lowered Self-Concept

Studies indicate another factor affecting bonds in stepfamilies is self-concept. This may be lower in stepchildren than in children from intact families. Various explanations have been offered. For example, some children devastated by the loss of a parent, may not want to try again with a new parent only to lose that one as well. Also, when parents do not discuss the divorce, some children may feel responsible for the breakdown and be guilt-ridden. Subsequent fears of not belonging or of being abandoned may follow. This is common especially in younger children. Losing a loved parent and gaining a second household in which they do not hold the same status as in the natural household may also contribute to reducing children's self-concepts. Lowered self-concept can then hinder a child's ability to desire and to attempt a bonding in a stepfamily.

151

Children's Ages

These factors intensify as the children get older. From the age of eight to twelve, bonding is most critical and most difficult. As mentioned previously, this is the time of emerging adolescence and identities. Many adolescents do not want to have to search for a family identity while they are searching for their own. Below the age of eight, a child may be "cuddled" and "loved" into security. But the older child often is not. The older child has been in a position of authority, which may be lessened after a marriage. Not only has the child lost that parent to another person, but has lost a treasured and needed position of authority.

Wise parents understand this need and help the child through the difficulty, while bonding at the same time. Both parents can sit down with the older child or children and thank them for the good job they did while Mom or Dad was a single parent. Praise them for their specific help and share with them how important their contribution was to the family's success. Add to these vital "warm fuzzies" a sincere desire for the child or children to have more time now to do some of the things that they may want to do. Explain that one of the things that both parents want to provide, as part of their new family, is to give everyone more opportunity to do things in which they are interested. End the explanation with a request that they still retain a few of the responsibilities that they formerly had. To take away everything conveys a message of "you are not needed any more." Not too many people, even children, like to feel that. Pick a few of the responsibilities that the child or children do well and that need to be done. Conveying to them that their efforts in those areas are still vitally needed and can add another layer of glue to the bond.

Spiritual Questions

Divorce can cast shadows of doubts on the spiritual condition of those seeking it. At least that is often conveyed by some well-meaning friends. When wounds are deep, Christian friends can help by applying supportive salve, not critical salt. This does not mean that the divorce process is supported or condoned. Nor does it mean that church discipline is not to be used. But it does mean that divorced Christians eed support to put their lives back in order.

This feeling carries over into the stepfamily. Children may view the new stepparent as an uninvited guest and be suspicious even of his or her spiritual intentions. One stepchild confronted the stepparent with the charge, "If you are so spiritual, why did you get divorced?" This does not seem to be the best way to start the spiritual bonding necessary in the step-family. Blending the family spiritually is the job for true Christian servants.

Christ said, "But whoever wishes to become great among you shall be your servant" (Matt. 20:26b, NASB). Becoming great in the stepfamily is by being a servant and not a dictator. The unknowing stepparent may assume dictatorial control in the step-family in an attempt to blend together. Edicts, orders, and new commandments come down from the new Mt. Sinai. Unsuspecting stepparents then try to force their new families to follow them to the "promised land" through the wilderness of blending together. Paul wrote especially to fathers, whether natural or step, "And fathers, do not provoke your children to anger; and bring them up in the discipline and instruction of the Lord" (Eph. 6:4, NASB). Provoking may come from dictating. Provoking may be the result of forcing. What then is "serving" a stepfamily and not "provoking" them?

Earning the spiritual respect of stepchildren takes time and being an example. It cannot be purchased at Sears. It comes through actions and not just words. Letting the message come through loud and clear that honesty and openess is the "name of the game" goes along with earning this respect. Don't shy away from the tough questions. Stick it out when the messy problems come up. Admit mistakes. Ask forgiveness. These are merely manifestations of a Spirit-filled life. What better way is there to win the spiritual respect of stepchildren than by being spiritual? Stepfathers earn the respect of stepchildren not by competing with a natural father, but by being another father. Stress the stepfather/ stepchild relationship. Don't compete with the merits or shortcomings of the missing father.

Mothers, too, have some special instructions: "But a child who gets his own way brings shame to his mother" (Prov. 29:15b, NASB). To be insensitive to the needs of children after a remarriage is typical. For many reasons, mothers immerse themselves in their new marital relationship and leave the children painfully alone. The preceding chapters have indicated other behavioral and psychological implications of this type of avoidance.

Stepmothers face some of the same problems as stepfathers. The hostile stepchild really does not want to be alone. A stepmother may feel that is what the child desires, but often that is not the case. Consistently trying to reach the child on the basis of being *another* mother and not a replacement is vital. Keep being the "right kind of person" and give God's grace the time to work.

Remembering that spiritual credibility takes time, both parents must work together to achieve this. This must be true in spiritual areas as well as in other areas of living. If one parent is spiritually stagnant, the effects on the rest of the family are evident. If one parent is slow to act on church involvement, the stage is set for further battle with the children. Both parents must act in unison. Both parents must take spiritual leadership. Both parents must be committed to involving the family in the church.

Church Problems

A problem may arise if different members of the family want to go to different churches. This is an acute situation when church preferences follow "party lines." Curtis and his two children had attended a sound church in their neighborhood since his divorce, while Ruth and her daughter had gone to their church for several years following Ruth's marital breakup. After Ruth and Curtis married, his two children wanted nothing to do with Ruth's church and Ruth's daughter felt nothing for Curtis's church.

Curtis and Ruth talked to a counselor at this

church about the situation. He gave them some sage advice, which resulted in their holding a family conference. During the conference, Curtis and Ruth said that they wanted to solve the church problem. Then they tactfully asked the children which church had the most to offer them in their spiritual and social lives. Before any final decisions were made, Curtis and Ruth led the children in a sincere prayer that God would lead them to the right decision.

Not asking for a decision then, Curtis asked the children to pray and consider both churches for a few days. Then they would get together again and decide. When the family reconvened, the situation was much less hostile. Curtis's two children decided that Ruth's church had more active youth programs and even had a Bible Club at school. They decided to try that church. Ruth's daughter thanked them for changing their minds and offered to introduce them to her friends at church.

In selecting the church, Curtis and Ruth considered the whole needs of the family. Employing the summit meeting approach, in an open, frank atmosphere, helped the children to see that this really was a family decision. When the children recognize this attitude, the door is open for solving some of the problems of bonding.

Sexual Questions

One last area of bonding that is more controversial than any other is in sexual areas. Sexual knowledge and growth is difficult and traumatic for children. Bringing in a new parent to the family can be chaotic. The intact family has the natural bonding of years of closeness and familiarity. The stepfamily has newness, doubts, fears, and even suspicions.

Seven-year-old Toby liked Mom's new boyfriend Frank. He was kind to him and often took Toby places. He even gave Toby some thoughtful presents. Toby really did not mind his being around Mom, but he "blew up" when Frank kissed Mom. Frank should not do that! Only his real dad could do that. Each embrace flooded Toby's mind with anger and questions. Why did Mom kiss Frank? Why did Frank want to hug Mom? If they got married would Mom have to sleep with Frank?

Thirteen-year-old Cathy just glared at her new stepmother, Katie. She even lashed out at her father one evening as he and Katie were heading up the stairs to bed. Her vicious attack questioned her father's moral integrity in sleeping with another woman. When her father explained that Katie was his wife, Cathy retorted, "Your wife is living elsewhere." Tears burst into Katie's eyes as she felt the anger and disgust of Cathy's emotions.

Children struggling to understand their sexuality often become more confused when they suddenly have to deal with their parent's sexuality. Nothing brings the dilemma on more quickly than for children to watch a natural mother or father go off to bed with another man or woman. Suddenly it comes to their realization that more happens in the bedroom than sleeping. Children may then wonder if Mom or Dad got married just for sexual fulfillment. If that is the case, then that is a selfish reason.

From this, children may deduce that since Dad or Mom care only for his or her sexual needs, then why shouldn't they? Their rapidly developing sexuality may then explode in the back seat of a car or in a home, when parents are temporarily gone. Also, a girl may rationalize that if "that woman" uses sex to get Dad's attention, then I'll use sex to get attention from someone, too. A boy may reason that if it is all right for Dad to sleep with someone else besides Mom, then it is all right for me, too.

These examples indicate the maturity level of children who are encountering their own sexuality. As they are discovering this sexuality in the comfort and security of their intact home, children may feel free to be open and candid with questions and concerns. But with a strange adult comes into the situation, this freedom decreases and insecurity increases. Perplexing questions may go unanswered in the home and researched in the locker room instead.

Bond Setters

Avoid Forced Bonding
No sure answer comes quickly. But some bonding guidelines are available. First, stepparents are wise to remember that they do not have the right to force familiarity and confidentiality with stepchildren. Be available and wait for the children to show acceptance and trust. Remember the years of closeness that promote familiarity and confidentiality are not there.

Be Available
Second, a natural parent is wise to share with

the natural children that they can come and ask questions at any time. Then, when a child comes to ask, challenge, or share, answer only those things about which they are concerned. Do not give dissertations. Wait for them to carry the discussion further.

Practice Discretion

Third, the new couple is advised to be discreet. To expose marital sexuality and physical immodesty in front of both step and natural children opens the door to some potentially explosive problems.

Respect Privacy

Fourth, stepparents are to respect the privacy of stepchildren. Marrying their fathers or mother is not blanket permission to invade their privacy. Knock before entering their room. Ask permission to enter a room where they may be dressing. In other words, respect their physical privacy in the same manner one would respect the privacy of a guest.

Explain Need Differences

Fifth, children need to understand that parents' needs are different from children's needs. Clearly and lovingly explaining that marital sex is part of God's plan for marital happiness places those needs in a spiritual as well as emotional perspective. This may help the children to understand that Mom or Dad will have sexual relationships with a new husband or wife. Understanding the difference between being a parent and a mate is a healthy by-product of this conflict.

Bonding Priorities

Bonding emotionally, physically, and spiritually happens at different rates in different degrees. Remarried people are wise to remember that the most important bonding is first that between the Lord and themselves. Second, the bond between them as husband and wife is God-ordained. The third bond with the children may or may not transpire. Allowing the absent stepchild bond to affect the bond that is there between husband and wife is a sure way to stunt "growing in step."

CHAPTER THIRTEEN
Engrave Them in Stone

One may wonder if Jacob felt the immense pain in his family as his twelve sons went through some of the problems typical in a stepfamily. As a matter of fact, Joseph and Benjamin, his two youngest sons, were full brothers who had difficulty with their ten stepbrothers. How much easier it would be if someone had written down long ago the ten commandments for stepparenting. Maybe it would have helped Jacob to avoid the pain and conflicts in his family.

Just as the Law provided direction over impulse, "stepparenting commandments" promote control rather than impulsive parenting.

Moses received the Law on Mt. Sinai where God engraved it on tablets of stone. Scholars have given many meaningful interpretations of the engraving in stone. But none may be as significant as the one that states that they are to be learned and embedded in a believer's mind, never to be removed. So, too, the two sets of commandments for stepfamilies, one for the stepparent and one for the natural parent, need to be embedded in the mind and never removed. In some cases they may be the only hope there is for the struggling natural or stepparent.

To "engrave them in stone" is to commit them as a way of life in the stepfamily. For in the stepfamily they surely will be tested and tried. Only if these guides are embedded in the mind will they survive to produce a "growing in step." So, get out your stone and chisel and start engraving these commandments.

Commandments For Stepparents

Commandment One: Love the stepchild. This seems obvious. Love is a staple of the Christian life, but still it can be the hardest attitude to produce in a strife-torn stepfamily. The basis of love is acceptance. That does not mean that a stepparent may feel all the warm emotions that may be present with a natural child. It just means accepting the stepchild(ren). Even though Joseph's brothers had sold him into slavery when God brought them back together, Joseph accepted his brothers.

Following acceptance comes love, but it starts with acceptance. Right feelings don't just happen, they follow right actions. And right actions come from the right kind of thinking. In the final analysis, right feelings come from right thinking. Right thinking is that the stepparent will accept the stepchildren and not expect them to be anything more than they are. This promotes the right kind of action toward the stepchildren. What follows is loving feelings. The formula is as simple as Proverbs 23:7a (NASB), "For as he thinks within himself, so he is."

Commandment Two: Avoid being cruel. Childrens' literature contains the stories of many cruel stepmothers. Cinderella's stepmother looked for ways to aggravate Cinderella's life. Remembering that it is always right to do right, the stepparent should avoid direct and/or indirect cruelty. Romans 12:17 (NASB) reminds stepparents: "Never pay back evil for evil to anyone. Respect what is right in the sight of all men." Being *fair* in discipline, *kind* in conversation, *thoughtful* in little things, and *unbiased* in treatment are some of the ways that stepparents may avoid being cruel.

162

But no greater cruelty can be experienced than that of being ignored and avoided by a stepparent.

Commandment Three: Don't usurp the natural parent's position. Often the stepparent becomes a relief pitcher. In baseball when a pitcher is removed it is up to the relief pitcher to bring home the win. So, too, the stepparent is often left with the responsibility of raising a family that he or she didn't start. Just as the relief pitcher in baseball is called out of the bullpen to finish something that he didn't start, the stepparent may be expected to fill that same type of role. He or she is not the natural parent. The natural parent may well be the one who is loved most by the children, but the stepparent may have to finish the work of raising the children.

With these built-in limitations, a wise stepparent doesn't try to replace or be the natural parent. Therefore, the stepparent is wise to wait for the stepchildren to elevate him or her to a position of a loved parent. If it doesn't happen, then the stepparent is still just another parent, a relief pitcher. But wait for the stepchild to do the promoting. The stepparent is not to stand in the way of children seeing, talking with, or loving their natural parent. Finally, the stepparent becomes involved in a "no-win" power struggle if he or she tries to outdo a natural parent in gifts, money, and/or time. Stay in relief and wait for the children to make the stepparent a starter.

Commandment Four: Fill in the missing elements. Filling in areas of need that a removed natural parent doesn't meet is like being last in line at the church fellowship dinner. What is left over will fill one up, but looking at what could have been is disheartening. Of course, it may not be fair to be the stepparent who gets to play taxi driver, or project advisor for the science project which is due in two days, but it is filling a needed parental function. Remember, for the stepparent, it is often the little things that grow into big things in stepfamilies.

Mike's natural father did all of the fun things with him, leaving stepfather Al with the hard things of teaching discipline and responsibility. As the years passed, Mike's love and respect for Al grew to the point that Mike asked Al to be the best man at his wedding. Al didn't compete with the natural father. He was content to fill in the missing elements and allow God to bring about the growth. It worked.

Commandment Five: No Gestapo tactics. In an attempt to get control of the family, Carmen became strict and rigid in her discipline of her husband's three children. What she envisioned as a smoothly running home became open guerilla warfare. And she was losing. Discipline and control are necessary, but Commandment One, love the stepchild, still applies. Too much control and discipline may be counter-productive.

Some obvious tactics that are guaranteed losers in the discipline and control struggles are motivation by fear, guilt, or threat. Others are manipulation, emotional coldness, avoidance, impatience, and brute force. These tactics may provide some temporary solutions, but they will often erupt in another brushfire later on in the day or week. They just don't work.

Commandment Six: Keep communication open. "Reach out and touch somebody" is a prevalent suggestion today. In stepfamilies, the only available

164

way to touch a child may be by talking, since sometimes physical closeness is not there. Important areas in which to communicate "touching" may be in those difficult ones regarding the divorce itself. Be open to discuss the divorce. Be open to discuss the feelings that children may have about the remarriage.

Keeping these lines open eases tension, not only between new mates, but perhaps between former mates as well. But do keep the communications open. Don't "hang up."

Commandment Seven: Be realistic. Stepfamilies have built-in problems. They don't just disappear. Stepparents too have built-in problems that don't just disappear. To avoid the emotional baggage that comes with remarriage is a sure formula for failure in the stepfamily. Accept these problems. Use the Lord to help carry those bags. Peter tells us: "Casting all your anxiety upon Him, because He cares for you" (1 Peter 5:7, NASB).

Commandment Eight: Be flexible. Christian bookstore shelves are filled with books that teach how to be flexible in marriage, in parenting, and in work. The same flexibility is required for stepparenting, perhaps even more so. New people with many and varied needs are suddenly meshed together in a new family. Further, accelerated needs for independence may occur among the stepchildren. At the same time, some of them experience increased dependency needs. In today's terms, it's a case of being "between the rock and the hard place." To handle this requires flexibility, maturity, and maybe professional help. Be flexible.

Commandment Nine: Don't fear counseling. "Where there is not guidance, the people fall, but in abundance of counselors there is victory" (Prov. 1:14, NASB). Those who have experienced stepfamily living and have survived often relate that special people helped them through the rough times. Carrying the burden alone may be a one-way ticket to trouble. During the rough times before and after a remarriage, seek counsel. Talk with a pastor. Speak with others who have remarried. Visit a Christian professional who is able to help guide the new family. Remember the issue is not how much I am supposed to know or am able to do by myself. The issue is victory — "growing in step."

Commandment Ten: Pick a mature mate. Jumping into a remarriage without carefully and prayerfully seeking God's leading cannot be a wise thing to do. As a matter of fact, it is a leading cause of remarriage problems. With all that may follow in the stepfamily, marrying an emotionally and spiritually mature mate is mandatory.

Commandments for Natural Parents

Ten commandments for stepparents are a good idea, but some are needed for the natural parent in the stepfamily as well. And they too should be engraved in stone.

Commandment One: Pick the right mate for the right reasons. Picking a mate for the wrong reason is why some remarriages end in disaster. Consider that the person is not only going to be a mate, but that he or she will have an impact on the children. They are relying on the parent to make a wise choice. Therefore, be wise in the choice of the next mate.

Commandment Two: Don't force the child/step-

parent relationship. Allowing the step-relationship to "grow in step" is a must. Forced growth is not conducive for producing firmly implanted roots. Allow the relationship to grow naturally. That is how a step-relationship becomes natural.

Commandment Three: Control the guilt. The guilt that often follows a marital breakup may become overwhelming. So subtle is it at times that a natural parent may not see that it is affecting his or her relationship with the children. Avoiding being motivated by guilt in dealing with the children is therefore vital to "growing in step."

Commandment Four: Be open with the children about the divorce. No one has so many painful questions to answer about the divorce as the custodial natural parent. Answer the children's questions in a truthful and non-vindictive manner. This will help them heal the pains still lingering from the divorce.

Commandment Five: Commit to a team effort with the new mate. Accept the new mate as the new partner. Act as a team in front of the children. Be a team before God. Live like a team emotionally and physically. This is a formula for victory.

Commandment Six: Don't sacrifice a new mate by favoring the children. A new mate is a mate for life. Children grow up and enter into their own lives. The first relationship lasts a lifetime, the second for only a few more years. Yes, they will always be offspring, but they will not always be children. Soon they will be adults. A new mate is always a mate. Make the commitment not to sacrifice a mate in favor of the children.

Commandment Seven: Know yourself. Asking

God to help you understand yourself is where understanding really starts. With self understanding intact, no emotions are off-limits. This stepfamily has a different bag of emotions to handle than the intact family. Therefore, knowing oneself and being emotionally mature enables a natural parent to be free to help the rest of the family "grow in step" emotionally.

Commandment Eight: Remember there's another natural parent. Remember that the children do have another natural parent. It is their right to pursue or not pursue that relationship. To prevent it or force it places unnecessary stresses on the stepfamily. Be wise and be fair.

Commandment Nine: Love the stepchildren. If the remarriage makes the natural parent a stepparent also, then love the stepchildren. A natural child senses that Mom or Dad really doesn't want or like the new step-sibling. If this happens, it may well turn the cold war into a hot one. Love the stepchildren.

Commandment Ten: Be a truth seeker. "And the truth shall make you free" (John 8:32b, NASB) said Jesus to the Pharisees. A natural parent will know the bondage-freeing experience of truth by seeking it. The issue is not which child is step or natural. The issue is, *What is the truth?* The issue is not which side someone is on, but what is the truth? The issue is not who wins the argument, but what is the truth? No greater commitment is necessary in a stepfamily than that of being a "truth seeker."

Now, put down your chisel. Look at the commandments. Keep them in your heart and mind. Ask God to help you use them in His grace. They may seem heavy at first, but they lighten as they help the stepfamily "grow in step."

"Growing in step" is certainly a complex issue. Some may think that it involves all growing and no harvesting. But a harvest will come. Just as God gave the Ten Commandments to guide believers, He also gives scriptural direction to the stepfamily to help them experience some of the bounty that he designed for marriages.

Be patient, be kind, be encouraging, be faithful, and be truthful. These are the spiritual fertilizers that will bring about an abundant crop of "growing in step."